Building Bridges During the Interim

A Workbook for Congregational Leaders

John Lepper

© 2012 Nurturing Faith Inc.

Published in the United States by Nurturing Faith Inc., Macon GA,
www.nurturingfaith.net.

Library of Congress Cataloging-in-Publication Data is available.

ISBN 978-1-938514-00-5

All rights reserved. Printed in the United States of America

Contents

Acknowledgements		iv
Introduction	A Message from Your Interim Guide	1
Chapter 1	Providing Leadership in Times of Anxiety	7
Chapter 2	Understanding the Congregation-Family Connection	19
Chapter 3	Saying Goodbye to the Past	33
Chapter 4	Appreciating Our Past	39
Chapter 5	Determining Our Identity	47
Chapter 6	Filling the Gaps of Leadership	55
Chapter 7	Relating to Our Denomination and Other Groups	65
Chapter 8	Seeking New Leadership	69
Chapter 9	Saying Hello to the Future	77
Epilogue	Dealing with Unexpected Situations	83
Notes		87
Resources		89

Acknowledgements

I am indebted to a number of people for their insights and assistance with this book. My wife, Connie, read the manuscript at various stages, offering suggestions for improvement. She and our daughter, Allison, took time to help make grammatical corrections. Their suggestions were invaluable.

Several other individuals offered guidance at various stages. These include: Israel Galindo, James Stillwell, Ron Higdon, Bob Johnson, Greg Alexander, Guy Futral, Jonathan Parks (son-in-law), and Al Lepper (brother).

I am particularly grateful for leaders in congregations where I've served as an interim pastor or provided a bridge to the interim.

Introduction

A Message from Your Interim Guide

Paul's prayer for the church at Ephesus is my prayer for your church: "I pray that out of his glorious riches he may strengthen you with power through his Spirit in your inner being" (Eph. 3:16, NIV).

I look forward to helping guide your congregation through the important interim period. Having served numerous congregations in this capacity, I have sought to help lay leaders build bridges during the interim.

An interim is a time of transition. Transitions are never easy and are often full of feeling and anxiety. Times of transition provide us with numerous challenges, some of which are:

- Saying goodbye to former leadership and to the past
- Coming to terms with the church's history
- Discovering or rediscovering the identity of the church
- Rediscovering and affirming the church's mission
- Dealing with shifts of power
- Dealing with conflict and how decisions are made
- Evaluating links to the denomination and similar groups
- Making decisions about procedures on selecting a new pastor
- Making a commitment to a new leader and a new future

Notes

The Big Four Bridge has been a Louisville landmark for a century. This half-mile span crosses the Ohio River connecting Louisville, Kentucky, and Jeffersonville, Indiana. In past years, hundreds of trains carried passengers and freight. Then, in the late 1960s, the bridge was no longer needed. But what do you do with such a huge bridge?

Owners disassembled and demolished each end, eliminating the approaches to the bridge. So for almost a half century, the Big Four Bridge has not really been a bridge at all.

Located in full view of many commuters and interstate travelers, near what is dubbed "spaghetti junction," local residents hardly notice it. But for those who see it for the first time, heads turn and comments are made: "Would you look at that! A bridge with the ends knocked off." Or, "Look! A bridge that goes nowhere."

The Big Four Bridge will soon see use again, but this time as a pedestrian bridge. Workers have now built an approach to the Kentucky side of the bridge.

The approach from the Indiana side must be constructed, and the deck of the bridge must be replaced to make a solid roadbed for cyclists and pedestrians. Once the bridge is open, those who cross will use various means. Some will walk, some will run, some will ride bicycles. Small children will be wheeled in strollers while others will be carried in arms.

Guardrails will be installed to protect those who use the bridge. Some seats along the way will allow pedestrians to rest or have leisurely conversation.

When the refurbished and converted bridge opens, it will not be the quickest way to cross the Ohio River. It will, however, provide a more personal connection between Louisville and Indiana.

The Big Four Bridge provides a kind of metaphor for the church's interim, or the time between pastors. Every interim needs an approach, or a beginning place, and a descent, or ending place. And just as the bridge over the Ohio River must be substantial and provide support for those who cross, the bridge between pastors must also be substantial. Perhaps the bridge between pastors also needs guardrails for protection and places to rest; places to have conversation and reflect. A parallel also exists in the slow movement of people on a pedestrian bridge with the slow, methodical pace needed to transition between the departure of one pastor and the arrival of the next.

The closing of another bridge in Louisville caused major disruption. The Sherman Minton Bridge, a double-decker bridge that spans the Ohio River between Louisville, Kentucky, and New Albany, Indiana, carried an average of 90,000 cars each day prior to its closing. It was deemed structurally unsound, so officials decided to close the bridge.

All drivers going east or west were rerouted around the city to a north-south interstate and bridge. With only two other bridges, there was no precise solution to this months-long commuting nightmare. Suddenly what was a twenty-minute morning commute lasted an hour, sometimes several hours. To cope, many people arose early in order to miss the traffic bottleneck. Some simply avoided the trek between Kentucky and Indiana; but for many, the commute was unavoidable. Thousands of people lived in one state and worked in the other.

Bridges are important, even during an interim. Bridges take work to build and to maintain. Crossing takes energy. Congregational leaders can construct a suitable bridge between one pastor and another, providing the structure that allows themselves and others to cross.

I have not been involved in building or maintaining any of the physical bridges I've spoken about, but I enjoy the fruit of others' labors when I point my car in the direction of the bridge. When the approaches on both ends are complete on the Big Four Bridge and the surface has been replaced, I will use my energy to walk across the bridge. After the Sherman Minton Bridge has been repaired and reopened, I'll enjoy crossing the Ohio River with much less hassle than is currently possible.

While I haven't been involved in building bridges of iron and steel, I have been involved in helping congregations build bridges between pastors. To date, I've served more than twenty-five congregations as an interim pastor or as a "bridge to the interim."

I've learned that congregations in an interim are in a kind of crisis, not necessarily in the sense that it is a time of intense difficulty or trouble, but rather in the Chinese sense of the word. The Chinese symbol for "crisis" is really two words: one symbol stands for "danger," and the other for "opportunity." It is the intention of this book to help congregations during the interim avoid the dangers and capture the opportunities.

An interim is a crisis in the sense that it is a time of decision. The Greek word for "crisis" means "decision," and the Latin root means "to decide." The interim is a decisive point. It is a fork in the road. A

Notes

decision—in fact, many decisions—must be made about the direction of travel. And it is not enough to take the advice of Yogi Berra who is credited with saying, "When you come to a fork in the road, take it." Sometimes decisions are more complex; transitions can have many variables.

From the time a pastor resigns until the next pastor steps into the pulpit, the congregation experiences a critical period. Some have called this period a kind of wilderness experience. It's a kind of chasm that needs to be spanned with a well-constructed bridge.

Some congregational leaders wish to build a bridge quickly and move forward to call a new pastor. Other congregations seem to wander, as in a wilderness, knowing they want to go toward the promised land but not really sure what steps to take.

A Book for Lay Leaders

As I think about the readers of this book, numerous names come to mind—Henrietta, Paul, Hugh, Jack, Gene, Janie, Sara. These names represent leaders in congregations where I've served during an interim. The target audience is congregational leaders. They may or may not serve on the search committee. They may or may not serve as deacons or elders. They are all lay leaders in their respective congregations, however. These congregations run the gamut from small country churches to larger city churches. Some have no ministry staff other than the pastor, and others are multi-staff congregations. Lay leaders who might find this book useful include:

- Church Council
- Elders
- The Session (Presbyterian)
- Consistory
- Leadership Team—by whatever name
- Deacon Body
- Personnel Committee

Purpose

The purpose of this book is to help lay, congregational leaders understand the dynamics of congregations during the interim. Lay leaders can make a difference in guiding their respective congregations through the interim. They can lead the way in building a substantial and healthy bridge between pastors.

Many years ago while sitting in a seminary class I made an observation about the path to a pastorate. My professor, Dr. Walter Shurden, replied: "Lepper, you can never predict what a pastor search committee will do." It's been almost four decades since I heard that comment, but I have repeatedly affirmed its truth.

Each search committee is different. The same is true of congregations during the interim. Interims are different for different congregations. Yet, most congregations during the interim have similarities. Interims differ in different congregations because each congregation has its own polity, history, demographic, size, and leadership.

This workbook seeks to help you, a lay leader, answer two questions regarding the interim:

1. What can I expect?
2. What can I do?

This resource will help you discern answers to these questions and provide helpful leadership during this critical time in your congregation.

Chapter 1

Providing Leadership in Times of Anxiety

A Message from Your Interim Guide

Congregations experience anxiety for a variety of reasons. Sometimes anxiety comes from outside the church as in a community or natural disaster. Sometimes anxiety comes from within the church, as with a building program or in a change of worship styles or of leadership. Now that your pastor has resigned, you are, no doubt, experiencing heightened anxiety. These feelings are inevitable and predictable.

I have felt such anxiety in the past as my own pastor announced his resignation. The experience was akin to a grief reaction. I remember such an experience when a pastor for whom I had a particular affinity resigned. I first experienced feelings of sadness and loss. Closely on the heels of sadness were my feelings of anger: "How dare he leave me and our congregation for another place?" In my head I could rationalize his departure, but in my heart I felt some rejection and maybe some feelings of abandonment.

I did not have a significant leadership position in that congregation, but I could imagine that leaders felt the anxiety more intensely than I. The whole congregation began to sense additional anxiety. Rational thoughts collided with feelings that were not rational, but present nonetheless.

On the following pages you will have an opportunity to sort out these thoughts and feelings as you determine what you can do to help your congregation.

A Bridge from Anxiety to Calm

As a congregational leader, you may have had some illusions regarding your position. Perhaps you thought as you accepted your current position, "I just want to serve Jesus." Perhaps you have been a long-time leader and have been through transitions before. In any case, you are now faced with anxiety in your congregation. You may feel this anxiety more acutely since you are a leader. Take some time to get in touch with your thoughts and feelings.

Now that our pastor has departed, what are my thoughts?

Now that our pastor has departed, what are my feelings?

Now that our pastor has departed, what can I do?

As a leader, your concern is with the whole congregation. One significant way to help manage anxiety is to follow pre-approved procedures. Early on, the congregation will need to answer these questions:

- What do the legal and/or organizational documents of the congregation or denomination say about transitions from one pastor to another?
- How will the congregation fill the responsibilities normally assumed by a pastor, such as Sunday-to-Sunday preaching and worship leadership, pastoral care, and administrative responsibilities?
- Is a certain leadership group in the congregation given the authority to appoint an interim pastor?

If a procedure is outlined in church documents, these need to be brought to the attention of the whole congregation.

Lack of communication can add to anxiety, so a major task of lay leaders during an interim is to communicate, communicate, and communicate. Think of the ways in which you are able to communicate, for example, the church newsletter and website, email, and announcements during worship or other meetings. Even a bulletin board can be used creatively. Recently a congregation that was searching for a pastor posted pictures of six or eight members, along with a quote from each person about his or her hopes for the next pastor.

If no clear procedures are in place, the first major task is to outline and agree on procedures, and then to inform and remind the congregation of these procedures.

Once the procedures have been agreed on, the congregation needs to decide on the nature and shape of the interim—specifically the shape of pastoral leadership.

Interim Options

There are several approaches to filling pastoral leadership following the departure of a pastor. These include various pulpit guests, an interim preacher, a traditional interim pastor, and an intentional interim minister. When the first three options are chosen, a search committee is often named soon after a pastor resigns and this committee begins work immediately to receive names and select a person to fill the vacant pastoral position.

Some congregations feel it is best to utilize a **variety of preachers** during the interim. The advantage is the congregation gets to hear different ministers during the interim. However, the disadvantage is that having no consistent voice in the pulpit can add to anxiety in the congregation.

I was a member of a congregation that chose this route, and it seemed to add anxiety to our congregation. Trust is a big factor. I was unsure of what to expect in each worship service, which increased my anxiety and diminished my trust.

I understand this problem is also prevalent in the business sector. When trying to fill a post of responsibility with no consistent "stand-in," no one leader seems to "own" that area of responsibility. Anxiety among remaining leadership can become intense. Both in church and in other

Notes

contexts, strong leaders might depart because of the unsure nature of the institution.

Although usually called an interim pastor, an **interim preacher** mainly fulfills pulpit responsibilities. The deacons and/or ministry staff provide for pastoral care duties such as hospital visitation. An interim preacher provides consistency in the pulpit and also helps in worship planning and leading in various other worship responsibilities such as communion and baptism. This option has some advantages, particularly if there is a staff member who can be responsible for other day-to-day administrative and pastoral care needs. It also seems to work when lay leadership is organized and has the expertise to provide for these needs. This approach has the potential of allowing staff and/or lay leaders to grow and mature during the transition.

A **traditional interim pastor** is often a part-time role and includes preaching responsibilities along with some pastoral-care responsibilities. Sometimes a traditional interim pastor may have administrative responsibilities such as supervising staff and meeting with the deacons and other committees.

An **intentional interim minister** has received training in helping a congregation to deal with five specific tasks by leading the members through a self-study. These tasks are:

- coming to terms with history
- examining leadership and decision-making concerns
- looking at denominational and other external relationships
- clarifying the congregation's identity
- committing to new pastoral leadership and to the future.

An intentional interim minister usually serves as a full-time pastor and is paid accordingly. However, this arrangement can depend on the size and needs of the congregation and also the minister's availability. This person usually leads in the following ways:

- The minister develops a covenant with the congregation as to what he/she will do and what the congregation will do. The covenant generally states that the minister will serve in a preaching/pastoral role and also lead the congregation in a self-study. The congregation agrees to engage in this self-study before forming a search committee. The compensation, including reimbursement for travel and housing arrangements, is outlined in the covenant.

- The minister sets up a transition team and works through this team to help the congregation engage in a self-study of the five tasks/components listed previously.
- The minister leads in a self-study that takes about nine months. This time allows for healing to take place. Generally, the actual search following the self-study takes less time than in traditional interims because the preliminary work of discovering identity, direction, and the kind of pastor a congregation needs has already been done.

The Center for Congregational Health is one of two certifying agencies for intentional interim ministers. This organization partners with various denominations in providing training for traditional as well as intentional interim ministers. For more information, see healthychurch.org.

Dealing with Anxiety

You, as a lay leader, can help those in your congregation deal with anxiety as they pay attention to the ways in which decisions are made. Anxiety is reduced as people become aware that there is a plan for moving from one pastor to the next and as people are assured leaders will follow this plan. Anxiety is reduced as lay leaders help the congregation overcome this initial hurdle of agreeing on the kind of interim ministry needed and as the interim minister is selected. The following paragraphs will help you understand how anxiety is minimized in other ways.

"Anxiety alone will not endanger a system [your congregation]. How anxiety is addressed will determine outcome more than anything," says Peter Steinke in his book, *Congregational Leadership in Anxious Times*. He issues the marching orders for leaders during an interim: "The leader will need to challenge the congregation, anxious souls as they may be, to use anxious times as a springboard for change, learning, and different functioning."[1]

Before I go further, let me clearly state my assumptions here. Anxieties run high during interims. Leaders cannot directly change the anxiety in the congregation. Leaders can, however, make a significant difference in congregational anxiety by calming their own anxieties.

Notes

Providing a non-anxious presence

Family Systems theorists Murray Bowen, Edwin Friedman, and Peter Steinke suggest one of the best things a leader can provide is what they term a "non-anxious presence." In my experience, I'm not sure a NON-anxious presence is possible. Instead, I strive for a LESS-anxious presence.

Friedman uses the example of a step-down transformer. Power on the electrical lines outside is too strong for use in our homes. Somewhere on a pole near your house hangs a transformer. This transformer steps down the power, making it useful as it supplies energy for lights and appliances. Friedman explains:

> To the extent leaders. . .can maintain a non-anxious presence in a highly energized anxiety field, they can have the same effects on that field that transformers have in an electrical circuit. They reduce the negative energy in a field by the nature of their own presence and being. . .The trick is to be both non-anxious and present. . .A major sign of being better differentiated is when the leader can be present in the midst of emotional turmoil and actively relate to key people while calmly maintaining a sense of the leader's own direction.[2]

The emotional current in congregations sometimes becomes overcharged. Heightened anxiety is triggered by various causes. You, as a leader, may not be able to disable the triggers for anxiety. But you can become a step-down transformer. By managing your own anxiety, you can begin to bring about calm in your current setting. Peter Steinke says this:

> The non-anxious presence is an anomaly, never a full-blown reality. It is intended to be a description of a way of being, the capacity to
>
> • to manage our own natural reactions;
> • use knowledge to suppress impulses and control automatic reactions;
> • keep calm for the purpose of reflection and conversation;
> • observe what is happening, especially with oneself;
> • tolerate high degrees of uncertainty, frustration, and pain;
> • maintain a clear sense of direction.[3]

Steinke further suggests that humans can be reactive (acting without thinking) but that humans also have the capacity to take time for more thoughtful responses. You cannot always control your initial impulses, but you can control your outward expressions.

Anxiety and stress seem to characterize the lives of many people in the world and now, during this time of transition, anxiety is heightened in your congregation. Self-control is listed as a fruit of the Spirit in Galatians 5:23. Self-control in the biblical sense means the inward power or the strength to hold on.

Nelson Mandela has been called the closest thing we have to a secular saint. He served for twenty-seven years as a political prisoner. After he left, he led the fight to overthrow apartheid in South Africa and was elected president.

In 1994, during the presidential election campaign, Mandela boarded a tiny propeller plane to fly down to the killing fields of Natal and give a speech to his Zulu supporters. When the plane was twenty minutes from landing, one of its engines failed. Some people on the plane began to panic. The only thing that calmed them was looking at Mandela, who quietly read his newspaper as if he were a commuter on the morning train to his office. The airport prepared for an emergency landing, and the pilot managed to land the plane safely. After they landed, Mandela got in the backseat of his bulletproof car taking him to the rally. He turned to his friend and said, "Man, I was terrified up there!"

Mandela was often afraid during his time underground, during the Rivonia trial that led to his imprisonment, and during his time on Robben Island. "Of course I was afraid!" he would tell friends later. It would have been irrational, he suggested, not to have been afraid.

On Robben Island, where he was a prisoner, there was much to fear. Prisoners who were with him said watching Mandela walk across the courtyard, upright and proud, was enough to keep them going for days. He knew that he was a model for others, and that gave him the strength to triumph over his own fear.

That's one example of self-control. The biblical image of self-control is wrapping your arms around yourself and holding yourself. Self-control means providing for yourself a safe place and providing this safe place for others because of a deep awareness of the presence of Christ in your life.

As a leader, you need to be aware of your own everyday tensions that are a normal part of life. You can refrain from dumping your anxiety on others. You can resist adding to the existing anxiety and tension.

Notes

Notes

The prophet Isaiah knew about anxiety. He lived during a time of great crisis. King Uzziah had been one of the most successful and energetic kings of Judah, and according to 2 Chronicles 26:3, he reigned for fifty-two years. His popular and solid reign ended badly, however, as he became arrogant and proud (v. 16). Scripture tells us: "In the year that King Uzziah died I saw the Lord sitting upon a throne, high and lifted up; and the train of his robe filled the temple" (Isa. 6:1, ESV). It was the year of national calamity. Isaiah had known no other king but Uzziah. Then one day Uzziah sinned, and was banned from his throne. It was a year of national grief. No doubt, people were anxiously wringing their hands. Isaiah found his way to the temple and became aware that, in a deep way, God was still in control.

Prayer is like that. True connection with God is a reminder, down deep, that God is in control. Remembering that God is ultimately in control, your anxiety is reduced.

Your self-control and calm can help stabilize a tense situation. You can choose to be a "step-up" transformer or a "step-down" transformer.

Beginning with yourself

When something happens, thoughts immediately come into our heads. Immediate thoughts are not calculated; they just happen. These thoughts are filtered through our past experiences as well as our own knowledge. So the first thing you, as a leader, can do is reflect on your thoughts, feelings, and needs.

What are your thoughts now that your pastor has resigned?

What are your feelings now that your pastor has resigned?

How do you feel about being in your particular place of service during this specific time?

As a leader and a congregation member, what are your specific needs at this time?

Where are you in your spiritual journey?

Strengthening your soul

It is said that when early Wesleyan Christians got together in small group meetings, their first question to each other was: "How is it with your soul?" When you accepted your current leadership position, you probably did so with a sense of self-giving, a sense of servanthood. In times like these, when anxieties increase and emotional currents run high, when you are called on to accomplish so many tasks, you may feel more like a service provider than a servant leader.

What would help you regain (or maintain) joy as Christ's servant?

How can you face your current task and reduce your own anxiety?

    Ruth Haley Barton suggests the pattern of Moses as a good example for contemporary leaders. Moses had private encounters and conversations with God. He talked, but he mainly listened to God. Following the private encounters, Moses moved to carry out what had been revealed to him. Barton says, "He did not seem to have any great strategies for leadership except to seek God in solitude and then carry out what God revealed to him there."[4]

Notes

Notes

How has it been with you lately regarding your encounters with God?

Perhaps your last pastor was the kind of preacher who fed your soul. Perhaps corporate worship has been your source of spiritual nurture. But now worship services in your congregation have changed and you may find your soul lacking in sustenance.

Some years ago I found myself in a kind of spiritual desert. I attended worship but didn't gain much. For those of us who attend seminary, sometimes our theological education becomes an encumbrance to, rather than a facilitator of, spiritual growth. That was the case for me. I was taught to be analytical in my thinking. I took the next step to be critical of leaders. No wonder I felt undernourished. About that time I sought out a spiritual director. During those weeks and months of spiritual conversation, I came to realize that other people were not responsible for my soul, my spiritual vitality. As my thinking changed, I began to take responsibility for my soul. Interestingly enough, I became less critical of other leaders.

Perhaps different personalities have different needs regarding solitude. As an extrovert, I gain energy from being with people. Introverts, however, gain energy from being alone. Both extroverts and introverts need time alone with God. Time with God strengthens our souls.

Perhaps a daily time of reading and reflecting on Scripture feeds your soul. Maybe it is a quiet time of centering prayer, a method of contemplative prayer that places a strong emphasis on interior silence. You may find strength in journaling or in corporate worship. A spiritual guide or spiritual director may help you quench your spiritual thirst and find strength in your soul. Hebrews 10:24-25 tells us: "And let us consider how to stir up one another to love and good works, not neglecting to meet together, as is the habit of some, but encouraging one another, and all the more as you see the Day drawing near" (ESV).

What personal spiritual practices feed your soul?

Every leader needs a quiet place, a place where his or her soul finds strength. This soul-strength provides the foundation for leadership. Congregations can be filled with anxiety. Leaders cannot directly control anxiety in their congregations, but they can control their own anxiety and, in turn, make a difference in that group of people.

What steps are you taking to control your own anxiety?

Summary

This chapter began with the assumption that congregations during an interim experience heightened anxiety. Leaders can make a positive difference by helping their congregations understand and follow pre-established procedures. Leaders can understand various options for an interim. While leaders have no direct power to diminish a congregation's anxiety, leaders can begin with themselves and engage in spiritual practices that nourish their own souls. In so doing, their self-control can bear fruit by stepping down the anxiety in their congregations.

The next chapter looks at how families and congregations are similar. A comparison will be made with families and congregations. The effects of crisis on families are similar to interims in congregations. With this understanding of family systems and the effects of crisis, a prescription for congregations during the interim will be provided.

Notes

Chapter 2

Understanding the Congregation-Family Connection

A Message from Your Interim Guide

As we think about your church in an interim, we are thinking about people in relationship—not just how individuals respond to the interim. When talking about loss for an individual, we think about what's going on *within* that individual. When we think about changes in a church due to the resignation of its pastor, we need to consider the question, "What's going on *between* church members?" For this reason, family systems thinking can help us in our understanding of how churches function before and after a pastor resigns.

Clarifying our assumptions about how family members relate will shed light on how church family members relate. Here are three assumptions:

1. The family is more than the sum of individual family members. A church cannot be understood simply by combining the personalities of individual members. We'll be looking beyond individual church members to the ways in which a congregation relates, communicates, and solves problems.

2. Families develop unique patterns of response. Beginning with the formation of a congregation, churches develop certain ways of dealing with its life together. These patterns include, among other things, how decisions are made, how differences are handled, and how emotions are expressed.

3. Some family patterns are constructive, while other patterns are destructive. Churches have an amazing capacity for creativity and also a remarkable capacity for destructive behavior. Acceptable patterns of relating, more than individual personalities, determine a congregation's destructive or constructive characteristics.

A Bridge to Understanding Families

Just as each individual has a personality, each family has unique characteristics. So too with churches: each individual member contributes to the congregation, and each congregation has its own characteristics. The following are some characteristics (from a family systems perspective) most families possess. These characteristics have similarities to church families.

Balance

Families are like hanging mobiles. When one part of the mobile is blown by the wind, other parts move to help the mobile regain balance. When a family member becomes ill, gets in trouble with the law, gets a promotion, or has a baby, the family gets out of balance. When this occurs, other family members compensate. The change, whether good or bad, creates an imbalance that, in turn, causes other family members to try to restore the equilibrium.

The same thing happens in congregations. When a pastor resigns, a congregation gets out of balance. Church members begin to compensate, seeking to regain the equilibrium.

How has your congregation maintained balance following the resignation of your pastor?

Rules

Whether secret or open, written or spoken, families live by rules. Behavior and relationships of family members are governed by rules. In his book, *Family Ties that Bind*, Ron Richardson says, "Rules are a set of expectations about how people should conduct themselves in various kinds of settings and circumstances. Rules say what is allowable and not allowable. They also say what the consequences are when the rules are obeyed or disobeyed."[5]

Rules are as important to the daily routine of congregations as they are to families. Rules help members know what acceptable and unacceptable behavior is. Sometimes rules are spoken, and other times they are unspoken. Most people on the inside of the congregation understand the rules, whether spoken or not.

Spoken and agreed-upon rules develop over time as congregations grow and mature. Official documents provide the written and consensus rules.

What are some written and unwritten rules of your congregation?

When a family undergoes a crisis, rules are often interrupted, or at least disrupted. Families in crisis search for new rules, or seek to regain or reinterpret old rules. So too, a congregation facing the departure of its pastor may have a disruption of rules while searching for new rules to guide the members.

Have you noticed a disruption of your congregation's "rules" following the resignation of your pastor? If so, it what way?

Hierarchies

Structures of authority come about so that families have a way of making decisions and accomplishing tasks. In this way, the family avoids chaos and unpredictability. The norm for families is for the older generation to have authority over the younger. Structures of authority can vary in their rigidity. Some families are rigid in their hierarchical structure. Other families are more flexible.

In the same way, congregations have structures of authority as a way of making decisions and accomplishing tasks. Some congregations have a congregational form of church government, while others have a more hierarchical polity. Even within denominations, congregations develop their unique patterns of decision-making and patterns of authority.

Notes

Notes

How would you describe the patterns of decision-making and authority in your congregation?

Whether in a family or congregation, when crisis occurs, structure is thrown off balance. Families that are not flexible to change have great difficulty coping when a crisis upends family structure. Perhaps the same can be said of church families.

In families, rigidity can contribute to an existing crisis and even precipitate a crisis. Rigidity can apply not only to the role of authority (and leaders), but also to a church family's overall response to a crisis. A family or church family can be "stuck in one gear" as the members respond to situations. When this single response fails, the congregation has difficulty adapting. Inability to have a flexible response leads to increasing fragmentation for rigid families and church families.

Emotional triangles

Triangles are a natural part of family life. An emotional triangle is any three-way relationship and can center on people and/or issues. Emotional triangles evolve in families and relationships as a way of coping with stress. When tension increases in a two-way relationship, another person or issue is pulled in to reduce the tension. Examples of family triangles are: two parents and a child, parents and a child's misbehavior, a husband and wife and his/her drinking problem, a husband and wife and his work, or a husband and wife and a family crisis.

In a kind of mysterious and often unconscious way, triangles can come about as a way of taking the focus off a particularly stressful issue. For example, a couple may focus on a child's misbehavior as a way to avoid dealing with their own relational problems. Or a child may "triangle" with one parent, aligning himself or herself with this parent in order to get that parent to "take sides" about a particular issue. Television soap operas thrive on lovers' triangles: stress and dissatisfaction exist between the persons involved, so one of the parties gets involved in an extramarital affair.

In all of these examples triangles temporarily ease or absorb tension in relationships but, in the long run, serve to increase family problems. David Cox describes triangles in this manner: "Individuals become triangled when they become the focus of the unresolved issues of two others, or when they get caught in a position of being responsible for the relationship of two others or another and the person's symptom or problem."[6]

Triangles happen all the time in congregations. Pastors can easily get drawn into a triangle with one church member, taking sides in a particular issue. Israel Galindo in his book, *Perspectives on Congregational Leadership*, points out those triangles are endemic and almost endless. He lists these common triangles in a congregation:

- pastor-spouse-pick-the-issue (one partner's sense of calling, family of origin issues, finances)
- pastor-children-church
- pastor-staff-congregation
- pastor-deacons-vision for the church
- pastor-staff person-another staff person
- pastor-the position of leader-former pastor who refuses to leave the church.[7]

Have you observed triangles in your congregation? If so, can you name some?

Closeness/distance barometers

Humans seem to have two opposite needs: togetherness and separateness. Families also tend to have a closeness/distance barometer or norm. Some families are so close and dependent on each other, they seem stuck together. Family specialists call this "being fused or enmeshed." These family members are so close, it is difficult for individuals to identify their personal feelings. They have difficulty thinking of self, and only see the "we" of the family. In other families, members are more distant from one another. These families may live in the same house, but in different emotional worlds.

In times of crisis, neither extreme—extremely close or extremely distant—provides the needed support for its members. Families that are fused may blow apart during a crisis. Families that are distant do not have the emotional support closer ties could provide. Families made up of well-differentiated individuals are more likely to withstand a crisis. By well differentiated, I mean a person who has some

Notes

Notes

emotional maturity, is not emotionally reactive to situations, and is able to be close to another family member without being absorbed into the other person's feeling state.

Congregations have a closeness/distance norm. Some church families are so distant, they don't really know one another. They meet for Bible study and worship, but don't really interact. Other congregations are so "into" each other's business, they are fused. And, as in families, congregations with leaders who are well differentiated are better suited to face the loss of a pastor with grace.

How would you characterize the closeness/distance norm in your congregation?

Effects of Crisis on Families

Congregations that experience the departure of a pastor have similar characteristics to families experiencing a crisis. Crisis brings change, disrupts routines, limits control, triggers disturbing emotions, alters communication patterns, and causes time pressures and increased fatigue.

Change

The most prevalent effect of a crisis on families is change. When I was a teenager, my mother's hospitalization, and later her death, brought dramatic and lasting changes to my family. Other, less significant crises also bring about change. Parents of two small children experience change when both children are ill. One or both parents must stay home (or at the hospital) to care for the children.

Crisis and change come home to a congregation during an interim. The congregational system is disrupted by the departure of a pastor. The church family is forced to make adjustments. While church members may long for life in the congregation to get back to "normal," members begin to realize that the pastor's departure means the congregation will never be like it was. The congregation must find a new normal.

How has your congregation been disrupted by the departure of your pastor?

Disruption of routine

A family's routine is disrupted when it experiences a crisis. Families in crisis often feel as if they are living in a holding pattern. How true of congregations, too! Equilibrium begins to return when an interim pastor starts serving. But even then, it sometimes feels as if life as a congregation is on hold. Anxiety can begin to rebuild after a lengthy interim as members begin to wonder if life will ever return to "normal."

How are routines different in your congregation now that your pastor has gone?

Lack of control

A family crisis leaves families with a sense of being out of control. A crisis causes families to lose control over people, relationships, and events. It's as if the crisis controls our lives.

Congregations in an interim may begin to feel that "the interim period" is in control. Church life must go on, but sometimes church members—especially leaders—may feel governed by the interim.

Has the interim limited your control? If so, how?

Disturbing emotions

A family crisis often triggers unpleasant emotions. These emotions may include anxiety, guilt, regret, and anger. Following the departure of your pastor, your emotions may catch you by surprise; your emotions may be uncomfortable.

Some church members may become angry with others they sense could have caused the departure of a beloved pastor. Other church members, who were more distant from the pastor, may be surprised by the intense emotions of others. These may not understand the grief reaction

Notes

of others who were much closer to the pastor, and may wish they would just "get a grip and move on."

Has the departure of your pastor stirred emotions in you? If so, name these emotions.

Altered communication patterns

Stress brought about by a crisis often changes the way a family communicates. Sometimes a family may depend on a certain member as a link in receiving and sharing information. If this person is absent due to a crisis, patterns of communication can become strained.

How true in congregations! Pastors are often the "gatekeepers" of information. Or to put it another way, the pastor may be the "communication hub" through which information passes. When the pastor departs, church members must quickly learn new communication patterns. Unless new ways of sharing information is learned, the lack of information and/or miscommunication can add to disruption in a congregation.

How have communication patterns been altered in your congregation?

Time pressure and fatigue

A crisis can intensify time pressure on families. The time pressure can also lead to fatigue. Congregations during the interim continue to have the same needs as before; but in addition to the energy needed to "do church," this congregation has the additional need of finding a pastor. Leaders may find themselves stretched as they serve on more than one committee or ministry group. Those who serve on a search committee may find themselves fatigued as they are called on to do double duty. One congregation with which I recently worked had gone through an extended interim of two years. The search committee had been active for those two years, most often meeting weekly. The husband of the search committee chair said as the interim ended, "I'm glad to get my wife back."

When navigating times of crisis, "family" meetings can be beneficial to congregations.

Congregational Meetings

Following you will find suggestions for congregational meetings. To be effective, those present at these meetings need to follow certain guidelines. Pause for a moment and consider several key components of a congregational meeting: purpose, facilitator's role and guidelines or etiquette.

Purpose

The purpose of congregational meetings is to allow all members of the congregation an opportunity to participate in a "church family" discussion. These meetings are not intended to be "open mike" night when everyone speaks to the entire congregation. Instead, in these meetings, people meet at tables in small discussion groups and each group appoints someone to summarize the discussion of the group. A facilitator initiates the process, but does not provide information.

Facilitator's Role

- Introduce the session and frame the conversation (questions, topic).
- Post guidelines on poster board or cards at each table.
- Guide the discussion.
- Help group members stay on topic.
- Monitor time.
- Guide groups to share information.
- Summarize contents of the discussion.

Guidelines/Etiquette

- Contribute your thinking.
- Listen to others in order to understand.
- Be respectful of differing views.
- Focus on ideas not people.
- Speak only for yourself.
- Be concise with your comments.
- Be respectful of the time.
- Allow time for all to speak.
- Stay on topic.
- Save tangential comments for later.
- Allow time for quieter group members to participate.
- Guard your tongue.

Notes

- Avoid making hurtful comments.
- Guard your anger.
- Don't use this as an opportunity to vent.

We will revisit the idea of congregational meetings and specific topics for discussion in the following pages.

A Prescription for the Interim

Congregations are all different, but all congregations have similarities. They function a lot like families. Congregations have a tendency to move toward balance. They have rules and structures of authority. Triangles are a given when it comes to relationships—within our families and within our church families. Congregations, like our families, tend to have a closeness/distance norm.

The effects of a pastor's departure on a congregation are similar to those of a family in crisis. Congregations in an interim are in the midst of change. Their routine is disrupted; they may sense a loss of control; they may have disturbing emotions and experience increased fatigue. With this knowledge, how can a congregation use this interim as a time to strengthen the body of Christ?

What follows is a prescription for congregations during an interim. It does not assume the congregation is sick, but rather offers a proactive way to avoid illness and stay healthy.

℞ #1. Pull together.

Warning: Danger ahead. Pull together or be pulled apart. A crisis is fraught with dangers and opportunities. A crisis can pull us apart or bind us together. Leaders provide a role model for the entire congregation as they pull together.

What are some ways your congregation is pulling together?

Suggestion: Hold a congregational meeting and discuss ways your congregation can pull together.

R #2. Encourage open and clear communication.

Warning: Poor communication and miscommunication add to disruption within the congregation. As odd as it may sound, church disruption can provide an opportunity to grow in your ability to communicate in positive and helpful ways. Good communication includes sharing information as well as feelings. Congregations whose communication is so characterized find themselves in a better position to solve problems related to the interim. Open and clear communication increases problem-solving effectiveness.

What are some examples of open and clear communication in your congregation?

Suggestion: Hold a congregational meeting and discuss ways your congregation can encourage open and clear communication.

R #3. Go with the flow; practice flexibility.

Warning: Turbulent waters ahead! Reminder: Rowing against turbulent waters is counterproductive. If you are in a canoe or kayak and the waters get rough, the strength of your rowing will not counter the force of the water. You can, however, use the force of the water to your advantage. The same is true in the turbulent waters of an interim. By going with the flow of the stream, you can guide the congregation toward its goals and a positive future. You cannot undo or overpower the turbulent stream. The best you can do is to be flexible and take advantage of the power of the disruption.

How have people in your congregation been flexible during the interim?

Notes

Notes

Suggestion: Hold a congregational meeting and discuss ways your congregation can go with the flow and practice flexibility during the interim.

R #4. Identify and use assets wisely.

Warning: Focusing on liabilities in order to blame or find fault can be counterproductive. On the other hand, looking at the assets of your congregation—especially human assets—can provide a positive way forward. Discovering the unique talents and abilities of your congregation is a first step. Once you discover individual gifts, take the next step by constructing a plan of action on how those gifts and talents can blend together.

What are five assets of your congregation?

Suggestion: Have a congregational meeting to identify and claim the assets of your congregation.

R #5. Draw on spiritual resources.

Warning: Humans who stand in their own strength may see no need for God's strength. The prophet Isaiah said, "But those who wait for the Lord shall renew their strength, they shall mount up with wings like eagles, they shall run and not be weary, they shall walk and not faint" (Isa. 40:31, NRSV). Notice the admonition to wait. Our haste to find a quick answer sometimes limits God's ability to exercise power. The word "renew" in this verse literally means, "to exchange." The sense is that humans exchange their weakness for God's strength.

How has your congregation drawn on spiritual resources?

Suggestion: Have a prayer meeting. In fact, have several prayer meetings. Remember that prayer involves talking to God and also listening to God. Use the time to pray for needs in your congregation and also to listen to God. Encourage members to pray for their congregation during their daily quiet time.

Summary

This chapter began by discussing ways congregations and families are similar. Congregations, like families, move toward balance and also develop rules, hierarchies, emotional triangles, and a particular closeness/distance barometer.

The chapter outlined some effects crises have on families and suggested that the departure of a pastor tends to have the same effects on a congregation. In both situations, crises bring change, disrupt routine, limit control, trigger disturbing emotions, alter communication patterns, and cause time pressure and increased fatigue (particularly for those with additional responsibilities).

The chapter concluded with a prescription for congregations during the interim, including suggestions for congregational meetings. This prescription does not assume a congregation is sick during an interim; rather, the prescription is preventive medicine. Congregations can enhance their health by pulling together, encouraging open and clear communication, going with the flow (practicing flexibility), identifying and using assets wisely, and drawing on spiritual resources.

The next chapter looks at the importance of saying goodbye to the departing pastor. Closure, or resolving this loss, is important to the well-being of individuals. It is doubly important to the well-being of a congregation.

Notes

Chapter 3

Saying Goodbye to the Past

A Message from Your Interim Guide

A congregation facing the time between the end of one pastorate and the beginning of another is entering strange territory. The interim has been compared to the biblical time of wandering in the wilderness after the flight of the Hebrew people from Egypt.

A sense of uncertainty and confusion may be present. There may be pronounced anxiety that prevents people from focusing on the present. As with the Hebrew people in the desert, there may be murmuring and complaining.

It is not unusual for there to be wounds left from disagreements between the departed pastor and individuals or groups of members. There may be hard feelings preventing people from looking forward to better days.

How do people of faith find their way through such thickets of feelings? How does a worshipping fellowship come to grips with its sense of self and its reason for being?

The answer is, "You *can* get there from here." From the closing of one significant chapter in a congregation's life to the opening of the next, wholeness and harmony are possible. An interim is a time of refocusing, of getting our bearings. This refocusing isn't easy, but it is possible.

With God's help, I encourage you to look back and appreciate the rich history of your congregation. I encourage you, specifically, to say goodbye to what has gone before. This includes saying goodbye to your last pastor. Now I realize you've already said goodbye. But I'm thinking about goodbye as a process, which includes not only literally saying "goodbye," but also saying goodbye in an emotional sense. We'll be talking more about how this is done in this chapter.

A Bridge from the Past

Saying goodbye is hard work. But though it's difficult, saying goodbye has its rewards. It's necessary to say goodbye in order to better say hello. I'm talking about more than the physical goodbye. I'm talking about those emotional ties that bind us to people, organizations, and ways of doing things.

Recall the day your son or daughter caught the school bus for the first time and headed to kindergarten or first grade. Things were never the same after that. It would be easy to cling to those memories and want to freeze your child in childhood, but you learned to say goodbye to that period even as you embraced your child's future.

From the moment you learn about your pastor's departure, you begin the "grief work." But until he or she walks out the door for the last time, your grief is anticipatory. What is known about grief, both anticipatory and following the loss?

Grief work

Elisabeth Kubler-Ross introduced her pioneering study of grief in the book, *On Death and Dying*. She interviewed terminally ill patients and arrived at five stages of grief. These same stages of grief relate to the anticipation of any major loss, even the loss through resignation of a pastor. The stages are summarized as follows:

1. *Denial* is often only temporary, but provides a way to soften the blow of anticipated loss by disregarding the actuality of the event.
2. *Anger* produces a feeling of wanting to blame someone or to voice unfairness or rejection.
3. *Bargaining* involves hoping the individual can somehow postpone or reverse a decision.
4. *Depression* is the stage of sadness when we begin to accept the certainty of loss.
5. *Acceptance* comes when we emotionally come to terms with the loss.

When a pastor resigns, the congregation experiences the loss as grief. The closer you are to your pastor, the more intense your grief. Though each church member's grief is unique, this loss, as with any grief, flows through a normative process. Those who work with grieving people say it is normal for the grief process to last from eighteen months to two years, sometimes longer.

While Kubler-Ross and others talk about grief in terms of stages, it's not always so clear-cut. Grief work is a process, and you might deal with various parts of these "stages" at any given time.

The initial reaction to learning of the departure of a pastor may be shock. This is particularly true if the resignation is unexpected. Depending on your closeness with your pastor, you may then feel numb. You may begin to experience a flood of emotions. You may cry. You may experience guilt and anger—sometimes simultaneously. You may feel guilty and wonder what you could have done to prevent your pastor's departure. If you said unkind words or had confrontations with the pastor, these memories may come to the forefront. You may be angry with your pastor for abandoning you. You may have anger but not be able to identify its source or target. You may have some anger at God. You may feel loneliness regarding this loss. Your sense of loss may be triggered as you encounter events without the pastor (such as worship services or needed hospital visits).

When you experience loss, you need time to work through the mix of emotions. Grief is work. When you deal with the loss rather than dismissing it, you begin the process of acceptance.

Each person experiences loss differently. Nevertheless, dealing with loss is a process, and it is normal to experience a variety of emotions. The fact that you are a Christian does not provide immunity to grief, nor does being a Christian allow you to bypass the normal emotions related to loss. The loss of a pastor by resignation probably will not cause as intense a grief reaction as the loss of a family member through death. Nevertheless, you will do well to squarely face whatever emotions you have regarding this loss.

How would you express your sense of loss following the resignation of your pastor?

Notes

Notes

Goodbye work

The two most important words a congregation says to a minister are hello and goodbye. The manner in which you say goodbye to a pastor will color how you say hello to the next pastor. The manner in which you say hello will color the ministry of the new pastor. Saying goodbye is more than a one-time interaction. It is a process that may take months.

Church families, like our biological families, have "multi-generational transmission." Israel Galindo explains:

> The Bowen Systems Theory concept of multi-generational transmission in families, although often difficult to accept at one level, is logically appreciated at another. Families pass along habits, traditions, beliefs, grudges, feuds, genes, and emotional process down the generations. That force can be as powerful as a tidal wave, or as subtle, though influential as an undercurrent. Most of us can readily appreciate how past generations affect contemporary family systems and the individuals in it. However, I find that many have difficulty appreciating the same for a congregation. This is despite ample evidence of how congregations get stuck, or have conflict, over issues in the past generations (even from many generations past). Generations and members have come and gone since 'the incident,' yet new members, who have no direct experience or connection with (and sometimes no awareness of) the issue, will find themselves acting out the same conflict.[8]

How you say goodbye to your pastor can become a major "incident" that lingers under the surface of the life of the congregation. What's beneath the surface can buoy the congregation if the goodbye was a positive (or healthy) goodbye. When the goodbye was difficult, the undercurrent can cast a negative tone on the congregation's culture.

Congregations say goodbye to their pastor in a variety of ways. For more than a decade I helped lead a three-day workshop twice each year for ministers and their spouses who were in difficult transitions. Some ministers were terminated outright, some were under pressure to resign, some moved on to other ministries, and some resigned with no ministry position available. The goodbye phase for these ministers was very difficult.

Strong emotions surfaced as these people shared their painful stories. Hurtful things were sometimes said by church members and friends. On occasion, the termination was so abrupt the minister and family were not allowed to come back to church and say their goodbyes. Even when they had opportunities to say goodbye, these became strained and sometimes lacked the usual parting rituals such as gifts or receptions.

I have also worked with scores of congregations following the departure of their pastor. Many of these departures did not end well. The pastor may have been asked to resign by the church leadership or a select group of leaders. Even when there is no moral failure, these strained separations continue to have residual emotional bearing on the congregation.

My friend David Odom, former president of the Center for Congregational Health, suggests there are four groups of people in the congregation when a pastor departs. There are those who feel a closeness and fondness toward the pastor and pastor's family. There are those who feel no such closeness and are glad to see the pastor go. Others have no strong feelings either way. And then there are those who don't know the pastor has departed. Perhaps the two groups with strong feelings—positive warmth or negative dislike—are the groups in the congregation who have the most "goodbye work" to do.

A friend of mine who is a minister, but not on a church staff, recalls the resignation of a pastor of whom he was particularly fond. "After P.D. left our church and the new pastor came, Sunday after Sunday I would feel angry as the new pastor preached. It finally hit me that I was grieving P.D.'s loss. After processing those feelings with my wife on more than one occasion, I began to accept the new pastor and invited him to play golf where we got to know each other."

This same friend also relates how his wife grew up in a small rural church that had successive student preachers. People in that congregation would eventually get attached to the pastor, but it was a very slow process because of the inevitable loss every two or three years—a normal process for them.

How did your congregation say goodbye to your pastor?

What particular events or rituals did you find helpful as you said goodbye?

Notes

Notes

Summary

This chapter stressed the importance of saying goodbye. While the departure of a minister may not be as intense as other losses, you need to pay attention to working through the mix of emotions and resolving your loss.

This chapter considered loss from a family systems perspective and introduced the concept of "multi-generational transmission." Congregations are like families in that they can carry emotional baggage from one generation to the next. Paying attention to the emotions that surface with the loss of a minister helps minimize carrying forward the negative issues.

The next chapter looks at a similar issue: appreciating our past. An interim provides members with the opportunity to dust off the congregation's trophy case and look at the ways God has blessed them in the past. It will also be a good time to look at how God has walked with the congregation during more difficult days.

Chapter 4

Appreciating Our Past

A Message from Your Interim Guide

Every congregation has stories to tell. Some of these stories are of success or joy. Others are stories of failure or grief. We have stories of the past, stories of the present, and stories of the future. It is good to pause during a time of transition to retell stories of the past.

If you were asked to tell about when you joined your church, what story would you tell? Who was pastor during that time? What was going on in the life of the church when you joined? If you were asked to tell about a specific time in which you felt God's presence in the church facility, what would you tell about?

I suspect that some stories would cause us to smile. Some might cause a tear, even a tear of joy. Perhaps some would be painful. I also suspect that if we heard each other's stories, we would be reminded that God was present, providing love and guidance.

One day you will want to think about your future story. You will want to shape a future vision of the church before you call a new pastor. But before you envision a future story, I encourage you to face backwards and remember how God walked with you in the past. Doing so will instruct your thoughts about your future.

The same God who walked with you in the past has a vision for your future. "'For I know the plans I have for you,' declares the Lord, 'plans to prosper you and not to harm you, plans to give you hope and a future'" (Jer. 29:11).

A Bridge via Storytelling

Congregations are rich with stories of their past. Stories can be found in written histories, but for our purposes, facilitating conversations about a congregation's past can be more rewarding than reading its history. Every member has a story, perhaps many stories, regarding his/her relationship with the church. I've observed these stories come alive during times of interim.

I have helped numerous congregations begin to share stories during the interim. This seems to work best in a fellowship hall, but it can also work in other spaces. Those present are asked to stand and arrange themselves around the perimeter of the room in the order of when they joined or first began attending the church. I then ask them to think about three questions:

1. When did you join?
2. Who was the pastor?
3. What was going on in the church during that time?

The facilitator of this conversation is challenged to help people tell their story and for others to hear the stories. With a large group, it's impossible to hear everyone's story, but you can hear representative samples. Begin with the oldest person or the person who has been a member longest. Then hear a story from newer members and those in between. Here are some of the stories I've heard.

Representative stories

"I first came to this church before the church was formed. We met in a 'tabernacle' for Vacation Bible School, and the 'tabernacle' was a makeshift building with a shelter and temporary walls. It had a sawdust floor. Following the Bible school, the church was constituted and Brother Taylor became the pastor. I was a rowdy teenage boy and Brother Taylor became my mentor, guiding me toward Christ and Christian values. I'll never forget the impact this had on me as a boy and how it's made a difference my whole life."

(a senior adult man)

"Our family came to this area when I was a small boy. We were Lutherans, but there was no Lutheran church in town so we attended this church the first Sunday. That following week the pastor came to visit us. We later joined, and our family has been in this church ever since."

(a man 80-plus years of age)

"I first came here just a few months ago. We have lived in the area for only a short time, and we were looking for a church for our family. The people here were so warm and receptive that we wanted to come back. We appreciate Brother Jim's messages and the fact that he visited us and welcomed us into the congregation."

(a young married man with small children)

"This community is very close knit, and this church has been the focal point for the community. I lived just outside the community, but came here because of the afterschool program when I was a child and teenager. This was the one place in my life that I felt accepted and affirmed. Even as a teenager, I said that when I grew up I wanted to move to this community. I now live just down the street from this church, and the church continues to be the center of my life."

(a middle-aged woman who works with youth)

"Like many people in this congregation, our family came here when our children were young. The war (World War II) had just ended, and we were all getting established. The church was a place where we, as adults, could have friends and a good place where our children could learn Christian values. If you look in the hallway in the back, you can see all the trophies of various sports teams the church sponsored. We had so many people then that our building was 'busting at the seams.'"

(an elderly adult)

"We are a bit different in that we just joined a few months ago. And actually, this was after the last pastor left. So we came here, not because of the pastor, but because we have felt so warmly welcomed by the church members."

(a middle-aged adult)

Notes

Notes

Importance of stories

The "line up around the room" time is a prelude to or an introductory phase of hearing each other's stories. This time provides opportunities for older members to get better acquainted with newer members.

Following this time of large-group sharing, I sometimes ask people to go back to their tables and continue sharing their stories of when they joined, who the pastor was, and what was going on in the life of the congregation at that time. On occasion I then take subsequent Wednesday or Sunday evenings to ask people to stand, by decade, and tell something about what was going on during that decade.

Stories need to be related, heard, and mined for their richness. According to *Narrative Therapy in Practice,* the stories we have in our heads and the stories we relate to others are a way of understanding and making sense of our experiences. Sometimes the dominant stories congregations have about themselves can be saturated with problems. If the dominant story (or narrative) is negative, the tendency is to continue living into that story.

But congregations have other stories and events that go unnoticed and untold. If an alternate, more positive story can be mined and discovered, congregations can begin living into that more hopeful story.

Stories about congregations are not just personal inventions. They are learned and repeated in conversations with significant people. These stories are then performed in our actions. The reactions of others to our actions and our stories become incorporated into our stories. Leaders in a congregation can begin to shape the dominant narrative by focusing on positive, hopeful stories. Here are some guiding questions that can help mine the stories:

What are your thoughts and feelings as you hear people relate these stories?

Are you hearing a theme as you hear these stories? If so, what?

How are things in your congregation different today than forty years ago (or during the decade being discussed)? If so, what?

Are there some values that have remained over time?

Did you notice similarities in the stories of members who have joined your congregation recently and members who joined many years ago? If so, what are they?

What do you appreciate about the stories of the longer tenured members?

What do you appreciate about the stories of the members who have been here only a short time?

The leader of these discussions is not so much a teacher as a facilitator of a conversation. As such, the facilitator might make conversation between various groups easier. For example, you might say, "Do those of you who have come to this congregation in recent years have any questions of members who have been here for a much longer time?" Or you might reverse it, saying, "Do any of you long-time members have questions of the folks who have come to this congregation in recent years?"

Just as families have various generations, so do congregations. Sharing stories is, at a minimum, sharing information; but stories are much more than information. People tell the stories closest to their

Notes

hearts; and these stories are almost always packed with emotion. Those present can connect on this deeper, emotional level. So then, conversations, such as outlined above, provide opportunities for generations to connect on an emotional level. We move from understanding to affirming and accepting. Sharing stories helps us achieve "the unity of the Spirit through the bond of peace" (Eph. 4:3b).

Another value of hearing stories is to remember how God has blessed in the past and how God has walked with the congregation during difficult times. An interim can be stressful; it can be a time of conflict. I remember helping one congregation when the pastor left under duress. The congregation was polarized, with one group glad the pastor left and another group (who had a particular affinity to the pastor) blaming this first group for the pastor's departure. So to say the least, it was a difficult time in the congregation.

This congregation met weekly on Wednesday evenings for a meal and conversations. A couple of weeks into this process, people had shared how they came to the congregation along with information about what was going on in the congregation during that time. These stories were shared at tables in small groups and then reported in the large group.

Those present began to listen as people told about various decades. An older member whom I would term a "patriarch" said, "You think we are having difficulty in the congregation right now. You should have been here during the fifties." He then began to recall some of the difficult circumstances and how the congregation had weathered those storms. He ended his statements by saying, "God saw us through those very difficult times, times more difficult than now, and God will see us through these times!" The power of his personality and the power of history added credibility to his words of hope. Those present could almost sense the healing begin to take place.

Returning to the beginning

Here's an exercise that will help you think about the beginnings of your congregation. In preparation for this exercise, find a printed history of your congregation. Look for a brief summary of the congregation's origins. If no printed history is available, write the summary yourself or ask someone to write it. At a congregational meeting:

- Set up four tables in an arrangement conducive to conversation.
- Ask participants to be seated at a table with other people.
- Distribute cards with the following assignments:
    1. **DANGERS** (What dangers were present during the early days of this congregation?)
    2. **OPPORTUNITIES** (What positive opportunities existed for this congregation during the early days?)
    3. **CHALLENGES** (What challenges did this congregation face during the early years?)
    4. **FEELINGS** (What might the early members of this congregation have been feeling?)
- Ask each group to listen for its assigned word/thought as you read several paragraphs about the beginnings of your congregation and to be prepared to talk for two minutes about its assigned subject.
- Allow time for discussion/compilation of ideas within each group.
- Ask each small group to report on its conversations to the large group.
- Following the reports, facilitate a conversation about the process by asking, "What were your thoughts and feelings as you engaged in this exercise?" Remind the participants that you are asking for their responses to the exercise and not new information about the content of the discussion.

Summary

The primary focus of this chapter is to highlight the importance of the past. Leaders can help their congregations build bridges to the future by remembering and celebrating how God has blessed them in the past. Every congregation has multiple stories about its past and present. These stories tend to be learned and repeated and lived out. Stories can be related, heard, and mined for their richness. Leaders can begin to shape the dominant future stories of their congregations as they help people focus on positive, hopeful stories.

In the next chapter, the focus turns to the identity of a congregation. In a mysterious way, the identity of a congregation is shaped by its pastor. The departure of a pastor provides opportunities for a congregation to rethink its identity.

Chapter 5

Determining Our Identity

A Message from Your Interim Guide

What is your "elevator speech" regarding your church? In other words, let's say you are waiting to get on an elevator and you strike up a conversation with another person who is also waiting on the elevator. This person discovers that you are a member of a church. Just as you both get on the elevator, the person says, "Tell me about your church." You have about 30 seconds, as you ride up the elevator, to describe your church. What would you say? My hunch is that your "elevator speech" would give clues to your church's identity.

What is the identity of your congregation? You exist in American culture and the specific culture of the community in which your congregation is located. What does that look like? How would you characterize the community in which your church exists? How has that influenced the identity of your congregation? How did your church begin, and how did that beginning shape who you are?

Pastoral leadership shapes the identity of congregations. In a mysterious way, the personality and style of the pastor are merged with the personality and style of the congregation. Perhaps a longer tenured pastor shapes a congregation to a greater degree. An interim is a good time to begin asking, "Who are we as a congregation? Who are we apart from our last pastor?"

A Bridge through Our Identity

Every congregation has its unique way of doing things. Every congregation exists in a particular community and a particular time in history. Each congregation has its identity.

Many factors shape identity. These may include such things as cultural context (both larger culture and the culture of the specific community where the church exists), historical context, denominational/theological orientation, personalities of individuals and families who make up the congregation, lay leaders and their styles, and pastoral leadership.

So the interim is a good time to ask, "What do we, as a church, look like now that our pastor has departed?" Even as you ask that question, you may begin to identify strong feelings of loss or even abandonment. Take a moment to consider and make notes in response to these questions:

Who are we as a congregation?

Who is our congregation apart from our last pastor?

The interim in a congregation is characterized as a wilderness experience. Perhaps you can identify with the experience of the Israelite people following their bondage in Egypt as they wandered in the wilderness. But if we think of the interim as a wilderness, let's not forget there was more happening in the wilderness than just wandering. The wilderness was the place the Israelites came face-to-face with God. It was a time of building a tabernacle and worshiping God. Moses was able to lead these people beyond their bondage and through those years because he had his own life experience.

Some time before God's people wandered in the wilderness, Moses had his own wilderness experience. On that particular day, Moses was taking care of his father-in-law's herd and noticed a bush was aflame, but the fire did not consume the bush. Moses turned aside and, in so doing, had an encounter with God that helped Moses affirm his identity and his future. God would use him as the person to lead God's people from slavery to freedom in a promised land.

Wilderness times can be times for churches to take a break and pay attention to their burning bushes. It can be a time of coming face-to-face with God and realizing God's intention for the congregation. Churches, like many of us in this culture, can get so busy with the day-to-day tasks of living that they don't take time to listen.

Notice that God chose to speak to Moses only after Moses paid attention. "And Moses said, 'I will turn aside to see this great sight, why the bush is not burned.' When the Lord saw that he turned aside to see, God called to him out of the bush, 'Moses, Moses!' And he said, 'Here I am'" (Exod. 3:3-4).

Think of the interim as God's gift—a time to turn aside and listen to God. A great challenge of the interim is discernment; it is a time we need to discern which future leader God is guiding us toward. But before we discern the leader, we can take time to discern God's special calling for our congregation. That may already be clear, especially to the leadership. But even if it is, the time can be used to allow the entire congregation to discern, share, and affirm that calling.

I'm not suggesting a full-blown long-range visioning process, but rather making time to turn aside so we can listen to God and notice what God is saying and notice who we are in relationship to our community and in relationship to God.

Consider taking three Wednesday evenings (or other times) to engage in discernment centered on various ways to listen to God.

Identifying context

Remember, your congregation does not exist for itself. Rather, Christian community—and that includes your local congregation—exists, as Daniel Vestal says "…to partake of and participate in God's reconciling mission to the world in Jesus Christ…Christian community is a means to an end. It is to represent, serve, and proclaim the kingdom of God…The purpose of Christian community is faithfulness to God's mission in the World."[9]

Much has been written in recent years about the missional church. A definition of missional church is often elusive and used to mean a variety of things. Alan Roxburgh has written numerous articles and books related to the missional church. He challenges congregations

Notes

to be on mission with God in the context of their own community. Sometimes congregations have the concept reversed. There are those who believe they are doing God's work in the congregation. Missional church literature calls congregations to think of God's mission in the world and how Christians might join God, not the other way around.

Understood this way, how would you answer this question: "What is God doing in my local community?" It's easy to look beyond your community to see how you can draw people into your congregation. Look instead at your community to determine how you might join God in God's work.

What is your congregation's historical, cultural, and community context?

Where do you see God at work in your community?

Recognizing the burning within

I have observed that our personal passions are often connected, in some way, with our pain. In my personal life, I have been drawn to help people sort through their personal and private issues as I provide pastoral counseling. During the time of sorting out this call and getting in touch with my own shadows, I came to realize my passion was connected to my pain related to the loss of my mother during my teenage years. During those days and even months of intense grief, I longed to have someone with whom I could just sit down and share my struggles. Unconsciously, my burning bush was to learn how to provide this solace and sounding board for others.

So maybe the first step is to sort out the individual passions of people in the congregation. You could do that during a Wednesday evening discussion. Allow time for people to share their passions and how these passions may be connected to their past pain. After a time of small group sharing, ask for a voluntary reporting of these stories. Record these in some way, either on a white board, newsprint, or via video projection, and then ask these questions:

What are you passionate about?

When considering the individual passions of people in your congregation, do you detect a theme? If so, what?

Are there groups of passions your congregation needs to listen to? If so, what are they?

You may have previously looked at individual gifts of people in your congregation (see page 30). If so, take a look at these again in light of individual passions. If not, now would be a good time to engage in this exercise. Identifying themes or clusters of gifts and passions begins to help you see the unique shape and texture of your congregation.

When considering the individual gifts of people in your congregation, do you detect a theme? If so, what?

What are the three or four clusters of gifts within your congregation?

Listening to each other

Now take time to turn aside and listen to God, perhaps by practicing the *lectio divina*. This ancient practice literally means "divine reading" and refers to a method of Scripture reading. Many Christians today use this method as a way of reading Scripture and then meditating and praying over its meaning. I am suggesting that you use this quiet approach as you listen to each other and to God.

Review the information from the previous discussions. You have thought about your specific context. You have had conversations about

Notes

people's individual passions, their unique gifts—the variety of assets of the members of your congregation. You have considered some unique corporate assets your congregation provides. Take some time to review these. Present them visually—on poster board, on video, in art—to your congregation. Allow this information to wash over your being, filling your head and heart. Consider the following questions while approaching this time in humility and quietness before God:

What emerges for you?

What do you hear God saying?

In light of what you have heard and felt, what do you discern God calling you and your congregation to do?

Moses did not see his own abilities as a leader because he focused on his weakness regarding his ability to speak. But God saw he had greater strengths, and the inability to be a public speaker was little cause to discount his other abilities. Take time to be silent before God as you sit around tables. Take time to pray and talk and discern. Listen. Listen. Listen. Then in a quiet spirit, share and learn and keep listening to God in the process.

What is God saying regarding your congregation's identity?

Where is God calling your congregation to involvement in God's work?

What is your congregation's identity, apart from your previous pastor or pastors?

What is God calling your congregation to be and do?

Summary

Congregations can build bridges to the future by claiming their identity. A variety of factors shape the identity of a congregation, including cultural context, historical context, denominational/theological orientation, and personalities of individuals who make up the congregation. Pastoral leadership also has a significant impact on the identity of a congregation.

An interim has been characterized as a wilderness experience. During this time, your congregation can take a break and pay attention to God's intention for it. An interim is a gift—a time you have to turn aside and listen to God, noticing what God is saying and noticing who you are in relation to your community and in relation to God.

The next chapter considers the subject of leadership and filling the gaps of leadership following your pastor's departure. Interims are complex times, and power struggles can result from a pastor's departure. Suggestions will be offered about how to face this issue squarely and chart the course through difficult waters.

Chapter 6

Filling the Gaps of Leadership

A Message from Your Interim Guide

Congregations in the interim are in the middle of numerous changes. And while change is not always easy to navigate, it is inevitable. One frequent change is a shift in leadership. A pastor's departure leaves a vacuum. Someone must step up and take care of day-to-day pastoral responsibilities, and others must step up and take care of decision-making. These changes of leadership can lead to conflict.

Leadership changes and power shifts usually occur during a pastoral transition. It is important that members of the congregation not panic when these changes occur.

There are a couple of positive actions a congregation can take to steer through these changes. One proactive approach is to examine leadership needs and the gifts that members bring to the congregation. Another is to focus on the congregation's mission, rather than becoming preoccupied with problems and transitions, and forgetting about the congregation's real purpose.

God has a vision for this congregation. God is in the business of transformation. God can use this time to transform the church. Your congregation, in turn, can become a transforming instrument in the community. I encourage you to understand and implement God's vision for yourself and for your congregation.

A Bridge though Lay Leadership

A pastor's departure provides a congregation with an opportunity to be the church. The writer of Ephesians suggests one of the roles of the pastor/teacher is to equip or prepare God's people for service in God's work. *The Message* paraphrases Ephesians 4:12 this way:

> He handed out gifts of apostle, prophet, evangelist, and pastor-teacher to train Christ's followers in skilled servant work, working within Christ's body, the church, until we're all moving rhythmically and easily with each other, efficient and graceful in response to God's Son, fully mature adults, fully developed within and without, fully alive like Christ.

This passage seems to suggest several things. First, the primary work of pastor is to equip the congregation for God's work. The work of the church is not totally dependent on the pastor but on the people. Mature Christians move in rhythm with one another, complementing each other's gifts so that God's work is done in an efficient manner.

Your work as a follower of Christ does not end as your pastor departs. Someone must step up and fill the gaps created by the pastor's absence. Perhaps the greatest complement to your departing pastor's leadership is for the congregation to accept the tasks at hand, doing the work of ministry. The pastor fills an important and vital role, but the congregation needs to move forward even during the interim. You have an opportunity to build a bridge to the future by fulfilling your role as a Christian leader in your congregation.

Responsibility and giftedness

Baptists, as well as other Protestant denominations, emphasize the concept of priesthood of all believers. Walter Shurden says:

> I was taught from the time of my conversion that all Baptist Christians are ministers. Baptists call this idea the priesthood of all believers. We got the idea from the New Testament, and it came to us through the Protestant Reformation, especially from Martin Luther. . .Baptist spirituality affirms through the concept of the priesthood of all believers that each individual has both the privilege or access to the presence of God and the responsibility

for the ministry of the Kingdom of God. Baptists have no special priesthood or clergy with exclusive privileges or responsibilities that do not belong to all the Baptist people. Each individual Baptist is a priest. The New Testament teaches it. The Protestant Reformers rediscovered it. And the Alcoholics Anonymous and the Baptists strive to practice it.[10]

While not minimizing the work of ministry outside the congregation, Shurden emphasizes the fact that a [Christian] priest "executes his or her ministry through the life of the local congregation of believers." What the local congregation does is critical to the work of each Christian. Worship, Christian education, and formation work together to motivate, encourage, and help each person and the body of Christ grow toward maturity. "Corporate worship," Shurden says, "reminds us that we are designed to be conduits and not catch basins of God's grace."[11]

Hear these words regarding the task of filling gaps of leadership: *let the church be the church!* But how does this work itself out in the nitty-gritty, day-to-day, week-to-week work of church during the interim? To answer this question, let me share my current experience.

I am writing this book while on a twelve-week sabbatical from my work as coordinator of Kentucky Baptist Fellowship (KBF). In my role as coordinator, I have overall responsibility for this non-profit organization. With more than seventy-five partner congregations, KBF has annual receipts of about $400,000, three full-time employees (including myself), and a thirty-six-member council (board). Our work includes networking, developing partnerships, providing resources for congregations, and engaging in missions.

As I prepared to take this sabbatical, my challenge was to set things in place so I could take a break from day-to-day responsibilities, oversight, and leadership in order to read, refresh, renew, and write. The leaders of Kentucky Baptist Fellowship took a look at those things that needed attention during my absence. We had conversations with people on the council and with employees, and agreed that the associate coordinator would fill the gaps. We became very specific with his additional responsibilities, as well as the scope or extent of his ability to make decisions. For weeks, each of us made notes as to what might need to be done during my sabbatical. Then we had a lengthy conversation and came to an agreement as to how tasks would be accomplished and how decisions would be made.

Notes

The same process can take place after a pastor's resignation and before his or her departure. The pastor and other church leaders need to make lists of the pastor's tasks and responsibilities. Perhaps there are documents, such as the pastor's job description, that need to be reviewed. At issue is the fact that pastors carry out their responsibilities in their own way. A job description cannot list all of the tasks a pastor accomplishes.

Most pastors give emphasis to one or another specific task, depending on their interests and unique gifts. They intuitively follow the leading of their inner compass, along with the Spirit of God, as the role is achieved. Much of a pastor's work is done in response to daily or weekly needs of a given congregation. Many of the tasks are just accomplished and go unspoken or unseen.

Now is the time to bring these unseen and unspoken tasks to the front. To assume they will just get done is unreasonable. In fact, to assume someone will fill the gaps without open and honest conversation may be an invitation to trouble. In any organization, whether non-profit or church or business, when the leader resigns, it is natural for someone to fill the vacuum of tasks and leadership.

Control and decisions

It is also natural for a power struggle to result when there are changes in leadership and the decision-making process. This can be a minor conflict as gaps in leadership are filled, or it can result in full-blown conflict.

We in the church often have strong convictions. Some members of the congregation may believe the previous pastor was leading the church in a direction contrary to their convictions. These people may take the occasion of the pastor's departure as a time to assert their influence, to bring about what they believe to be a corrective. Others in the same congregation may have had an affinity to the previous pastor and to the current direction of the church. These two groups may vie for control of decisions and leadership. Very strong-willed individuals can exacerbate conflict, particularly if the congregation is already polarized into factions prior to the departure of the pastor.

So what can a congregation do to prevent or minimize serious conflict as the pastor departs? The scope of this book does not include helping congregations that are engaged in serious conflict. Enlisting the services of a professional with experience in conflict resolution may be indicated if your congregation is experiencing serious conflict. You may choose an interim pastor who is skilled in conflict resolution. If you are involved in an intentional interim, your minister guide will help you through a self-study. One of the aspects of the self-study is examining how decisions are made.

Even congregations that are relatively healthy and are not in serious conflict can be proactive as they begin the interim. A first step is to follow what has already been suggested regarding conversations with the pastor and congregational leadership. Another proactive step is to look at church documents and procedures already in place. Talking openly about all of them will help each leader to be accountable and to work within the parameters of established norms.

Do you have a leadership team that is already in place? Some congregations have elders. Other congregations have a church council or committee structure. Now that the pastor has resigned, the structure of the leadership team may need to be tweaked a bit. In any case, the role of these leaders is invaluable. Their responsibilities need to be restated clearly—both within the group and in the whole congregation.

Revisiting a Prescription for the Interim

Now might be a good time to review the prescription for congregations during the interim found in chapter two. Look at these again as you think about leadership shifts. When so many people and personalities are involved, as in the case of congregations, nothing is simple and nothing ever works out as planned. Look at your congregation in light of these five prescriptions and ask, "How can we apply this to our congregation right now?"

℞ #1. Pull together.

The departure of your last pastor caused a vacuum of leadership and some reshuffling of responsibilities. But on the way to sorting out those roles, several leaders in your congregation may have found themselves in a power struggle. To say that your congregation needs to pull together may sound like an elusive goal—more like a dream than a real possibility. I'll admit: there's no pull-together-magic-wand. The very people who need to hear this may be locked in what seems to be a never-ending power struggle, and they would be the last ones to hear or heed. So what can you do?

Notes

Notes

There's no simple answer here. These situations need mature and discerning minds and responses. Remember that your attitude colors your approach, and a positive attitude can make all the difference. If you move forward with "guns a' blazing," you may add more anxious fuel to this fire. You as a leader will need to proceed cautiously. Remind the congregation about the need to pull together and of your goal to get through this interim and continue to move forward as a congregation. Perhaps you could have a congregational meeting in which members suggest ways to pull together. The leadership team will model pulling together as each member does just that. Begin with yourself. Approach discussions in a spirit of prayer and humility; pointing fingers can only exacerbate a tense situation.

What can I do to help my congregation pull together?

℞ #2. Encourage open and clear communication.

Have you noticed that conflict and poor communication seem to be linked? Lack of communication or miscommunication and conflict go hand-in-hand. The leadership team's role and responsibilities need to be clarified, restated, and communicated to the entire congregation. However, beyond communicating the role and responsibilities of the leadership team, information about decisions and direction needs to be communicated. Specifying avenues of such communication may be helpful.

A primary role of a leader—and this includes a leadership team—is to keep the constituency informed. The leadership team may be charged with day-to-day matters. This team will want to keep the congregation apprised of what is going on. Some decisions may be brought before the entire congregation for action. In such cases, the time and place of decision-making meetings will need to be clearly communicated. The congregation also needs to be informed about the issues at hand.

Clear and open communication will go far to alleviate assumptions, suspicion, and gossip—three symptoms of dysfunction.

In what ways is the leadership team in your congregation keeping the congregation apprised of what is going on in your church?

℞ #3. Go with the flow; practice flexibility.

Your congregation is living through a scene in which there is no script. In earlier days, when you had a pastor, you came to expect certain things. The way of doing things became a pattern, and you understood the pattern. Now there is no pattern. You, as a leader, can chart the go-with-the-flow course by the way you respond to these changes.

Leaders may not be able to control situations, but they can influence the tone. As with the previous prescription, there is no magic wand you can wave to get people to be flexible. However, you can practice flexibility yourself and become a role model in this regard.

What is the tone in your congregation right now?

Is there a spirit of anxiety in your congregation? If so, what evidence have you seen?

℞ #4. Identify and use assets wisely.

Hopefully you have identified assets of your congregation along the way. Your biggest asset may be people and their gifts. People have stepped up to accept leadership during this time. Another asset may be the ability of leaders in your congregation to work together, allowing synergy to build.

If you have not had an asset discovery congregational meeting, consider having one now. Attendance by the leadership team at meetings such as these is vital. Ask people to sit at tables, as before, and brainstorm the human assets of your congregation. Provide tear sheets and markers, and ask each table to appoint a scribe to record these. Celebrate the assets as each group gives a report. After reports are given, ask each group to brainstorm how the congregation may be able to use these assets more wisely. Hear these reports and, if needed, ask the leadership team to reshape how assets are being used.

What are three assets of your congregation?

What are some ways your congregation can use these assets more wisely?

R #5. Draw on spiritual resources.

Spiritual resources are the bedrock of congregations. Regular attendance is vital. That may sound mundane and even unspiritual, but just showing up for worship, Bible study, and other meetings may be the most spiritual thing you can do right now. I like what the writer of Hebrews said:

> Let us draw near with a true heart in full assurance of faith, with our hearts sprinkled clean from an evil conscience and our bodies washed with pure water. Let us hold fast the confession of our hope without wavering, for he who promised is faithful. And let us consider how to stir up one another to love and good works, not neglecting to meet together, as is the habit of some, but encouraging one another, and all the more as you see the Day drawing near. (10:22-25, ESV)

Now is the time to hold onto your belief in a good God who sent Jesus to cleanse us from sin. God is faithful, and we are called to be faithful to God and God's church. Now is the time to encourage each other, practicing love and kindness. Meeting together to worship and engage in Bible study and fellowship can significantly add vitality to your congregation. As with other aspects of this prescription, the leadership team needs to provide a role model. Attendance at meetings is a minimum requirement of a leader.

What specific spiritual practices help you personally?

What specific practices have been important to your congregation's well-being?

Summary

This chapter suggested some ways your congregation can be proactive in filling the gaps of leadership created when your pastor departed. Practical suggestions were offered, such as encouragement for church leadership to have intentional conversation with the departing pastor. Tasks and responsibilities the pastor has assumed will need to be reassigned to someone else—staff, lay leaders, or interim pastor. One way to pay attention to shifts of leadership is to revisit the prescription for congregations during the interim (see chapter two). This prescription also applies to the issue of leadership shifts.

The next chapter will look at how the congregation relates to its denomination and other groups. A congregation's relationship to its denomination is greatly influenced by the pastor. The interim can be a time to look at connections and ask, "How would we like to be linked to our denomination and to other groups?"

Chapter 7

Relating to Our Denomination and Other Groups

A Message from Your Interim Guide

No congregation exists alone. Congregations are part of a larger community, cultural and denominational context, and heritage. In some cases a congregation's connection to the larger church, and to other entities beyond the local congregation, is through the pastor.

Like many congregations, yours can be connected to the churches in your own community through an ecumenical ministerial association. This association of congregations may join together for worship during special occasions such as Thanksgiving, Holy Week, or Advent. They may also join together to provide benevolence for persons in need. Sometimes these joint efforts are ongoing, with a special fund for relief. At other times, these efforts may focus on special projects such as providing baskets of food at Thanksgiving or "Angel Tree" gifts at Christmas.

No doubt, your congregation is involved on some level in your denomination's local, regional, or state convention or organization. Sometimes this involvement is more clergy-based than laity-based. Your congregation may also be involved with parachurch groups such as Habitat for Humanity, Samaritan's Purse, or the Willow Creek Association.

Whether denominational, ecumenical, or parachurch, a congregation's connections to outside entities are greatly influenced by the pastor. In some cases, the pastor is the only link to these groups. Even if a layperson links the congregation to an outside group, because of the high visibility of the pastor in a congregation, the pastoral link naturally provides more visibility. So an interim can be a time for a congregation to look at its connection to its denomination and to other groups and ask, "Now that our pastor has departed, how would we like to be linked to our denomination and to other groups beyond our local congregation?"

A Bridge through Connections

Assumptions you have about connection to your denomination are based, in large part, by your specific denomination. Disciples of Christ congregations, for example, assume they will relate to the Region and will follow the procedures set forth in the Search and Call process. While congregational in nature, Christian Churches (Disciples of Christ) assume they will draw from a pool of candidates who have their ordinations approved by the larger church. American Baptist Churches follow a similar practice.

Other Baptist groups such as those who relate to the Southern Baptist Convention or the Cooperative Baptist Fellowship are even more congregational in nature. These Baptist congregations may have similarities regarding ordination and calling a pastor, but a national, state, or regional group does not set procedures about ordination and calling a specific pastor. The ways in which each congregation relates to its association, state, and national organization are based on the assumptions held by the congregation.

Heritage and specific denominational context shape how your congregation views connection. Baptists come out of the free-church tradition. For Baptists, local congregations are autonomous and self-governing. Historically speaking, Baptists have functioned with tension in this regard. Baptists affirm free-church/self-governing status while at the same time relating to associations beyond the local church.

Current connections

If you are involved in your congregation as a lay leader, you may already be aware of your congregation's polity and heritage regarding connections. You may be familiar with the specific connections your congregation currently has with outside entities. However, it may be that most people in the pew are unaware of these connections.

How do you obtain a greater understanding of the connections your congregation has with your denomination and other groups?

How do you help those in your congregation gain a better understanding about such connections?

You might begin by familiarizing yourself with your congregation's polity and its historical relation to the denomination. You can then help others in your congregation understand the nature of your congregation's polity, specifically as it relates to denominational connections. Sharing this information can be done through articles in the newsletter or bulletin or on the website. Understanding how your congregation is connected to outside groups might be one of many steps in minimizing anxiety and building cohesiveness during the interim.

Conversations with the departing pastor (prior to his or her actual leaving) would be an excellent place to begin understanding the current connections of your congregation. Ask the pastor to help the leaders in your congregation understand ways your congregation is connected. The pastor may have strong feelings about some of these entities and want the congregation to continue these connections.

What are some groups or entities, including your denomination, with which your congregation is connected?

How is your congregation connected with each of these groups?

Past connections

An interim is a good time to dust off the church's history to understand connections in the past. It's not necessary to conduct an exhaustive study of the history. Rather, consider having a series of brief presentations during worship or other appropriate times, such as Wednesday evening services, about your congregation's connection to outside entities. You could title these vignettes "Congregational Connections,"

Notes

and ask specific individuals to give three- to five-minute presentations about a variety of connections.

Following is a list of potential vignettes that may help you think of specific ways your congregation, either as a whole or through individuals is connected to outside entities:

- Our congregation's involvement in specific mission projects
- Our congregation's support of the denomination's camping program
- Our congregation's involvement in the founding of our local association
- Our congregation's annual offering for missions
- Our congregation's hosting of associational/state/regional meetings
- Our members who have served on ____ board or committee
- Our members who have served as workshop leaders in our association/state/region
- Our congregation's involvement with Habitat for Humanity
- Our congregation's financial connections to the denomination

Summary

Congregations have varying degrees of connection with their denomination and other outside entities. A congregation's connection (emotional and otherwise) is sometimes via its pastor. The interim is a good time for a congregation to become proactive in understanding its connections with outside entities. This awareness can lead to affirmation of what currently exists and also provide the knowledge that, in turn, will help a congregation shape its future desires regarding connections. Awareness and desires of future shape can be instructive for a search committee as the members look for a pastor who can fulfill congregational expectations.

Chapter 8

Seeking New Leadership

A Message from Your Interim Guide

Building bridges during the interim is more like crossing a river on a pedestrian bridge than crossing a river in your car on an interstate highway bridge. Your congregation has been deliberate in changing from one pastor to another. You did not speed toward the future but, instead, you walked forward and allowed everyone in the congregation to stay together.

You are now arriving at the place for which you've longed. You said goodbye to the last pastor. You considered who you are as a people, apart from your last pastor. You identified how God has blessed your congregation in the past and how God walked with you during times of difficulty. You are now ready to move forward. You are ready for a new pastor.

But we have two more deliberate steps before that is possible. The first of these steps is to review the interim and ask yourself if you are ready to call a pastor. The second is to carefully consider the kind of pastor who is needed to lead you forward. You want a pastor who respects who you are as a congregation and one who fits your unique situation. You want a pastor whose unique theology, style, and personality correspond in some way with the unique theology, style, and personality of your congregation.

Discernment is important; and information can instruct discernment. I encourage you to allow what you've done thus far in this interim process to inform you as you consider and discern the kind of pastor you desire to lead you into the future.

A Bridge to Our Destination

How many times have you heard a child ask, "Are we there yet?" "Countless!" you say. Perhaps this is one way I continue to have "childish" ways. I like to know (even if it is an approximation) how much more travel time I have.

Enter the modern marvel of a GPS. At first glance I never thought I would want a GPS. I travel quite a bit and enjoy reading maps. Like many men, I don't like to ask directions, but then, I'm not usually directionally challenged. I find myself regularly disagreeing with the directions of a GPS. So why would I need a one?

Then a few years ago I received a GPS as a Christmas gift and discovered quickly that the turn-by-turn directions to the destination are only one of the advantages of having a GPS. The feature I have enjoyed most is knowing how many miles and approximately how long before I arrive at my destination.

Your congregation has spent months now in the interim. At times you may have felt like you've been living life on hold. You may have asked yourself or another leader, "Are we there yet?" or "How much longer until we get a pastor?"

Today as I check the local news, one headline seems to blare: "Sherman Minton Bridge Repairs Half Complete." Commuters from Louisville and Southern Indiana have spent months in congested traffic, waiting on the bridge to be repaired. But they must wait a few more months before they can cross safely. Workers have completed many repairs, but they are not yet finished.

What about your congregation? Your congregation has been building a bridge from your last pastor to your next pastor. How are you doing in that regard? Let's take a few minutes and review the important tasks of this interim bridge and assess your progress.

Checklist for Bridging the Interim

Take a break from the journey across the bridge to the interim and assess your progress. Ask yourself these questions about your congregation as you determine your readiness to complete this journey.

What is the level of anxiety in your congregation?

How long has this kind of anxiety existed?

Have certain individuals or groups functioned as a step-down transformer, lowering the anxiety? If so, describe their actions.

Are there those who amplify the anxiety? If so, describe their actions.

What was it like to say goodbye to your last pastor?

Did you observe any rituals, such as a service of recognition or a reception, to say goodbye?

Have you as a group dealt appropriately with the grief of losing your last pastor? If so, how?

Notes

Notes

How have you remembered and celebrated the past during the interim?

If you took time during the interim to remember and celebrate the past, what were some values or benefits of doing that?

Did your congregation take time during the interim to consider its identity apart from the last pastor? If so, how?

Does your congregation have a clear picture of who it is? If so, what is it?

Did your congregation take time during the interim to reflect on and discern God's call? If so, what process did you follow?

How has your congregation handled shifts of power during the interim?

How were these shifts of power filled?

Did this process lead to undue conflict? If so, how?

Is your congregation "pulling together" during this time, or has the interim caused a "pulling apart"? Please describe.

How would you characterize communication in your congregation?
_____ *Open and clear*
_____ *Only a few people are "in the know."*
_____ *We tend to need someone to blame.*

Is your congregation practicing flexibility? If so, how?

Has your congregation identified its assets? If so, what are they?

How has your congregation drawn on spiritual resources during the interim?

Has your congregation reviewed how it relates to its denomination and other groups? If so, what insights did you gain?

Notes

A Leader for the Future

A friend of mine says that congregations have their own personalities and that, on occasion, congregations move to call a pastor when they hear "their sound," basing a decision on feelings and intuition and not reasoning. But congregations need to be cautious and do more than just listen for "their sound." Congregations need to consider carefully the kind of pastor needed to lead them. I have observed that congregations often tend to call a pastor who has strengths where the last pastor had weaknesses. Perhaps it's a natural tendency to do this.

I was working with a search committee some time ago and one of the members, a man who was in the real estate business, made some insightful remarks. First, he said that he and the committee were receiving pressure to find a perfect pastor. He said he was having a difficult time helping people understand there's no perfect pastor.

Then he gave an example from real estate. He said, "Let's say you are moving and that your current house has a leaky roof. You would probably pay very close attention to any house you were moving into and be sure the new house did not have a leaky roof. So you buy this new house, thinking you have finally found a perfect house. You live there for a few months only to discover that there are plumbing problems. So you come to a rude awakening that you haven't bought a perfect house, but rather a house with a perfect roof!" The moral of his story is self-evident. There is no perfect pastor, so we need to think of more than our last pastor's weakness in considering our next pastor.

A leadership group in your congregation needs to help the congregation think as objectively as possible about the kind of pastor needed. If a search committee has been named, this is the logical group to guide the process. Written surveys, congregational meetings, and small group conversations are three ways to achieve this goal. It is important to take into consideration the work done during the interim.

Your congregation has said goodbye to its last pastor. You have considered your congregation's identity apart from that pastor. You have celebrated how God has blessed your congregation in the past. You have charted a course through some rough waters as leadership (and perhaps decision-making) has shifted. You have considered how your congregation relates to the denomination and other outside groups. Now the big question of future pastoral leadership needs to be asked in light of all that information.

Members of your congregation continue to be anxious about finding the right pastor. Members will need ample opportunity to have a voice in that decision—even as a search committee leads the process. Draw on your denominational resources at this point. Sample surveys exist in abundance. These, as well as ideas for congregational meetings or small group conversations, can easily be obtained from your denominational office, print resources, and the internet. Your job will be deciding on how to proceed in gaining the kind of information needed without overwhelming your congregation. I suggest using at least two methods: verbal communication and a congregation-wide survey.

Summary

You have now answered the question, "Are we there yet?" The answer is, "Almost." You have reviewed the various tasks that have been accomplished during the interim. In doing so, you have determined the level of readiness for welcoming a new pastor.

You have considered how to allow every member of your congregation to have a voice in the kind of pastor your congregation calls. Results of surveys, congregational meetings, and conversations with small groups have been tabulated and reported to the congregation.

The hard work of building a bridge to the next pastor has been done. The additional hard work of searching for and calling your next pastor remains.

Notes

Chapter 9

Saying Hello to the Future

A Message from Your Interim Guide

Some time ago I received an email from a lay leader at a church in Louisville, Kentucky, where I had spoken on some Sunday mornings and led congregational meetings on Wednesday evenings in a program I call "Bridge to the Interim." The idea behind this bridge is to come in for about a month to help a church find its bearings and also find a longer-term interim pastor.

The email said something like, "We have found a pastor and were wondering if you could come back and help us again. You helped us with a Bridge *to* the Interim before and now that we have found a pastor, we were wondering if you could help us with a Bridge *from* the Interim?" It so happened I had three available weeks, so we arranged for the "Bridge *from* the Interim."

Leaders in this congregation thought it would be important to help the church think through how they might welcome a new pastor. I commend them for their foresight and desire to be intentional. After months of searching and expending much energy to find a pastor, it would be easy to breathe a sigh of relief. This congregation decided it was also vital to think about saying hello. This congregation gave me an opportunity to help the members think about the important aspects of saying hello.

A Bridge to the New Pastor

Paul's words to the early Christians in Ephesus, though lofty in nature, provide some worthy goals for churches saying hello to a new pastor:

> I therefore, a prisoner for the Lord, urge you to walk in a manner worthy of the calling to which you have been called, with all humility and gentleness, with patience, bearing with one another in love, eager to maintain the unity of the Spirit in the bond of peace. There is one body and one Spirit—just as you were called to the one hope that belongs to your call—one Lord, one faith, one baptism, one God and Father of all, who is over all and through all and in all. But grace was given to each one of us according to the measure of Christ's gift. (Eph. 4:1-7, ESV)

According to Susan Lanford in her book, *Remarriage and Blended Family Workshop,* three themes or tasks are present in blended or step families. These same three themes or tasks seem to be present when a minister becomes pastor of a congregation. These are:

1. To understand and be understood
2. To accept and be accepted
3. To affirm and be affirmed

Understanding relates to our thinking: a challenge of the mind. Acceptance relates to actions: a challenge of the will. Affirmation relates to the feelings: a challenge of the heart.

Understanding and Being Understood

Before you travel too far down the road of saying hello to your new pastor, remember that your hello is in some sense connected to your goodbye. Before you can say hello in a healthy way, you need to have mourned the loss of the previous pastor or interim pastor. The first chapter of this book stressed the importance of saying goodbye. Unless you resolve the loss of previous relationships, you can bring unfinished business to the new pastor. Failure to finish the grieving process can negatively affect new relationships. In the case of one church, the interim had lasted two years and the members had grown quite fond of their interim pastor. Remember:

- Loss comes in many forms…the loss of relationship with a previous pastor or interim pastor, the loss of dreams and expectations (regarding past leadership), the loss of support from the former pastor, the loss of a familiar preacher.
- The feelings of grief and sadness may surface, even when you think you've resolved a previous loss. Without facing these feelings honestly, they can emerge in harmful, destructive ways.
- The new pastor will have his or her own ways of doing things, and these may be different from those of the previous pastor or interim pastor.

The mental maps of others

A book with a clever title sheds light on the importance of understanding and being understood. Chapter one of *Too Soon Old, Too Late Smart: Thirty Things You Need to Know Now* provides good insight for congregations and their new ministers. In a chapter titled "If The Map Doesn't Agree with the Ground, the Map Is Wrong," author-psychiatrist Gordon Livingston tells about a time when he was a young lieutenant in the 82nd Airborne Division trying to orient himself on a field problem at Fort Bragg, North Carolina. As he studied a map, his platoon sergeant, a veteran who had taught many junior officers, approached to ask if the lieutenant had figured out where they were. The lieutenant replied, "Well, the map says there should be a hill over there, but I don't see it." The wise sergeant replied: "Sir, if the map doesn't agree with the ground, then the map is wrong."

Livingston says that over the years he's listened to hundreds of stories of how life has gotten off course. Over and over again, he says the issue is that we move through life trying to force the maps in our heads to conform to the ground on which we walk. Problems in relationships often result when the maps in our minds don't agree with the maps in other people's minds. This metaphor can be instructive for congregations and pastors as they say hello.

As humans begin any new relationship, understanding is a good starting place—specifically understanding each other's mental maps. The pastor and congregation begin this new relationship with their own histories, perspectives, and assumptions. For example, each member of the congregation has a mental picture about the responsibilities of a pastor, what we may call role expectations. Each member's role expectations differ because of different personalities, perceived needs, and history.

Notes

A job description and other written documents may help alleviate misunderstandings. But because it's impossible to write down every expectation, the job description forms only a summary of expectations. Prior to accepting this call, the new pastor and various committees and groups have conversations about expectations. These conversations guide your discernment and decision-making. You may perceive this new pastor can fulfill the expectations of the congregation, but the pastor brings his or her own gifts and mental construct of role and responsibilities. The new pastor may have a different perception of what it means to be pastor of your congregation.

Norms for the new church family

At this point in its life, your congregation has similarities to a blended or stepfamily. With the arrival of a new pastor, the congregation becomes, in effect, a blended church family. So as you think of this new family, consider the importance of norms.

The dictionary says that a norm is "…a standard or pattern, especially of social behavior, that is typical or expected of a group." You as a congregation already have norms, but the new pastor also has his or her way of doing things. Help the pastor understand the norms of your congregation. What is normal for you now is different than it was when your last pastor departed.

Deciding what is normal is an ongoing task of congregations and pastors, particularly in the first year or two. The norms will shift as a new pastor moves into this leadership role, a process that will require answers to questions such as:

- What will the norms of this congregation be with this pastor?
- Will the norms stay as they were before? If so, which ones?
- Will new people have a voice in determining the norms?

Accepting and Being Accepted

Understanding and being understood provide a foundation for long-lasting relationships. By understanding each other, new patterns are emerging. You are now moving to the next phase of saying hello: accepting and being accepted. Acceptance comes as trust is woven into the new fabric of church life. This is not automatic and often proceeds in starts and jerks. The developmental cycles of stepfamilies are instructive for congregations saying hello to a new pastor. Consider these stages identified by Susan Lanford in *Remarriage and Blended Family Workshop*.

Stage 1: Fantasy

Regarding stepfamilies, a couple sometimes remarries believing they can return to square one and make the perfect family they hoped to have the first time. This expectation is more often than not an illusion. Perhaps a perfect church family does not exist either—even though we sometimes believe it can happen. A perfect pastor does not exist either. At some point we must become more realistic. While a perfect church family and a perfect pastor may not exist, perhaps a healthy church family is attainable.

Stage 2: Confusion

The differences in preferences and expectations are now becoming apparent. Sometimes these can be articulated and examined. At other times the pastor and members may withdraw from each other and conflicts may emerge. When this happens, we can remain in the conflict mode or move toward resolving our differences.

Stage 3: Accepting Differences

We must accept the fact that differences are normal and inevitable, and that it is at this stage when we decide whether or not to unify as a pastor and church family. One place families (and church families) get stuck relates to how we manage differences. We may choose to control the other person, withdraw or cut off, attack, become passive-aggressive (gossip is a good example of passive aggressive behavior), engage in triangles, or accept differences. If your congregation successfully negotiates the differences hurdle, you can then move to the next stage.

Stage 4: Stability

Stability in a church family does not mean sameness without change. It does, however, mean the pastor and church members begin pulling together to face continual challenges and change. Conflict becomes the opportunity to learn more about differences and accept them.

Stage 5: Commitment

At this stage the pastor and congregation commit to remaining a church family, connected through good and bad times, distant and close times. Paul's words become real as members are "eager to maintain the unity of the Spirit in the bond of peace" (Eph. 4:3).

Affirming and Being Affirmed

At this point the pastor and congregation have arrived at understanding. You not only understand differences, but also have begun to accept differences. The next major step is to affirm each other in light of, and maybe in spite of, differences.

Affirmation is the fine art of focusing on or paying attention to what is right and then expressing appreciation for it. Affirming right actions or good decisions speeds the adjustment in blended church families since no one can automatically know which behavior is or is not acceptable.

Affirmation cannot be conjured up from thin air. It needs receptive soil if it is to grow. Affirmation can grow through these ways:

- Learn to celebrate daily and weekly victories, no matter how small.
- Begin to establish new traditions that belong only to this church family with this pastor.
- Keep careful track of new traditions and memories through times of sharing testimonies, stories, and life together.
- Engage in open discussions to set goals, and plan ways for every church family member to be involved in meeting those goals.

And now, a blessing for your congregation as it welcomes a new pastor:

> Through inspiration, perspiration, concentration, and by the power and grace of God, may your congregation and pastor become "one in the bond of peace."

Epilogue

Dealing with Unexpected Situations

A Message from Your Interim Guide

As I complete the writing of this workbook, an unfortunate and unexpected accident occurred in Western Kentucky. A 300-foot section of a bridge over Kentucky Lake was destroyed when it was hit by a ship too tall to pass under the structure. Thankfully, no one was injured. However, now people needing to travel from Cadiz to Murray must take a detour of about forty to fifty miles in order to reach their destinations. Upon first hearing about the bridge accident, I quipped, "It's been a bad year for bridges in Kentucky!"

In this workbook we have used the bridge metaphor as a way to think about the interim and how congregational leaders help provide a bridge between pastors. We looked at some similarities between physical bridges and bridges between pastors. "Every interim needs an approach, or a beginning place, and a descent, or an ending place. And just as the bridge over the Ohio River must be substantial and provide support for those who cross, the bridge between pastors must also be substantial" (see page 2).

But what happens when our efforts to build a substantial bridge between pastors meet with disaster? Maybe the bridge isn't completely destroyed, but perhaps it is rickety or full of potholes. The work of the church is never as ideal as we might like to think. Conflict happens. People get angry. Sometimes the heightened anxiety of the interim makes our best efforts seem ineffective. So what should we as congregational leaders do when the bridges we build seem to collapse (or, at a minimum, need repair)?

Notes

First, I suggest we avoid the pitfall of trying to make things happen. To do so moves us into the manipulative or controlling mode. Writing from a systems perspective, Israel Galindo suggests, "Willfulness does the harm."[12] By this he means that leaders do more harm than good when they try to impose their agenda on the congregation in manipulative and coercive ways.

We may not be able to help our congregation avoid all the hazards of building effective bridges, and we cannot control the anxiety of others, but we can manage our own anxiety and help bring about calm.

During times of heightened anxiety, even times when it seems our most valiant efforts count for nothing, we are not without recourse. I'd like to suggest three necessary dimensions for leadership during difficult times.[13]

Self-regulation describes the internal dimension of the leader's response to anxious situations. Heightened anxiety, often present in congregations during the interim, can lead to reactivity. Reactivity can, in turn, lead to poor choices. When this happens, leaders can focus on regulating their emotional reactivity. Like Isaiah and his experience in the temple, we can see the bigger picture of God's presence and, in so doing, we begin to regulate our own anxiety. We cannot, by force of will, calm the anxiety and reactivity in the congregation. However, our calm can provide a role model and influence those around us.

Self-definition describes the external dimension of the leader's response to anxious situations. The focus moves to how we communicate with others. We define self as we share our thoughts, values, and goals with others. This kind of self-definition does not mean "setting others straight" about what they should think or feel. It means, however, being in dialogue with others and revealing our thoughts and feelings, and listening to others as they share their thoughts and feelings. This can become a powerful tool when done in a calm, non-reactive manner.

Maintaining contact becomes the vehicle for self-regulation and self-definition. Self-regulation has little consequence if done in isolation. Self-definition implies relationship with others. To make a difference in our congregations, nothing can replace our presence. Building a substantial bridge between pastors is no easy task.

When our best efforts at building a bridge between pastors seem ineffective, our response may make a significant difference in our congregation. We may not be able to regulate the "anxiety-temperature" in the congregation, but we can work to regulate our own anxiety and reactivity. We may not be able to control the outcome, but we can control the manner in which we communicate our own thoughts, values, and feelings to others. Our self-regulation and self-definition make the biggest difference as we stay connected to our congregation.

Notes

Notes

[1] Peter Steinke, *Congregational Leadership in Anxious Times: Being Calm and Courageous No Matter What* (Herndon, VA: The Alban Institute), 7.

[2] Quoted in *Academic Leadership Journal*, 4, no. 4, posted Sept. 14, 2010, http://www.academicleadership.org/52/the_edwin_friedman_model_of_family_systems_thinking/.

[3] Steinke, 35.

[4] Ruth Haley Barton, *Strengthening the Soul of Your Leadership* (Downers Grove, IL: InterVarsity Press, 2008), 31.

[5] Ron Richardson, *Family Ties That Bind: A Self-Help Guide to Change Through Family of Origin Therapy* (Bellingham, WA: Self-Counsel Press), 12-13.

[6] Cox.

[7] Israel Galindo, *Perspectives on Congregational Leadership: Applying Systems Thinking for Effective Leadership* (Richmond, VA: Educational Consultants, 2009), 27.

[8] Ibid., 92-93.

[9] Daniel Vestal, *Being the Presence of Christ: A Vision for Transformation* (Nashville: Upper Room Books), 85-86.

[10] Walter Shurden, "Baptist Spirituality As I Have Known It for Half a Century" (lecture, Campbellsville University, Campbellsville, KY, Mar. 29, 2011).

[11] Ibid., 16-17

[12] Galindo, 189-190.

[13] Ideas for this section come from Lawrence Matthews, "Theology and Family Systems Theory in Dialogue" (J. C. Wynn Lecture, Colgate Rochester Divinity School, Rochester, NY, Nov. 5, 1998.)

Resources

Barton, Ruth Haley. *Strengthening the Soul of Your Leadership.* Downers Grove, IL: InterVarsity Press, 2008.

Galindo, Israel. *Perspectives on Congregational Leadership: Applying Systems Thinking for Effective Leadership.* Richmond, VA: Educational Consultants, 2009.

Galindo, Israel. *The Hidden Lives of Congregations: Discerning Church Dynamics.* Herndon, VA: The Alban Institute, 2004.

Gilbert, Roberta M. *Extraordinary Relationships: A New Way of Thinking About Human Interactions.* New York: John Wiley & Sons, Inc., 1992.

Hester, Richard L. and Kelli Walker-Jones. *Know Your Story and Lead with It: The Power of Narrative in Clergy Leadership.* Herndon, VA: The Alban Institute, 2009.

Lanford, Susan. *Remarriage and Blended Family Workshop.* Nashville: Sunday School Board, 1989.

Lepper, John. *When Crisis Comes Home: Revised and Expanded.* Macon, GA: Smyth & Helwys, 2009.

Nicholson, Roger S., Editor. *Temporary Shepherds: A Congregational Handbook for Interim Ministry.* Washington, DC: The Alban Institute, 1998.

Richardson, Ronald W. *Becoming a Healthier Pastor: Family Systems Theory and the Pastor's Own Family.* Minneapolis: Fortress Press, 2005.

Richardson, Ronald W. *Creating a Healthier Church: Family Systems Theory, Leadership, and Congregational Life.* Minneapolis: Fortress Press, 1996.

Steinke, Peter L. *Congregational Leadership in Anxious Times: Being Calm and Courageous No Matter What.* Herndon, VA: The Alban Institute, 2006.

Steinke, Peter L. *How Your Church Family Works: Understanding Congregations as Emotional Systems.* Herndon, VA: The Alban Institute, 1993, 2006.

Vestal, Daniel. *Being the Presence of Christ: A Vision for Transformation.* Nashville: Upper Room Books, 2008.

"*Building Bridges During the Interim* calls for congregations to find their spiritual center for a journey across a potentially dangerous stream of transition between pastors. This book is a gold mine of spiritual wisdom, practical astuteness, and systemic understanding. It provides realistic acceptance of the dangers of interim periods between pastors for a congregation while offering step-by-step blueprints for 'building a substantial and healthy bridge between pastors.' John Lepper artfully guides congregations to let go of their past, discover their identity, and build toward a place where by the power and grace of God, a congregation and pastor become 'one in the bond of peace.' *Building Bridges* is a call for spiritual renewal through congregational self-assessment and faith formation. This is a must read for church leaders of all denominations charged with shepherding a flock across the tumultuous transition between pastors."

G. Wade Rowatt
Professor of Pastoral Care and Counseling
Baptist Seminary of Kentucky

"The heightened anxiety in times of ministerial transition and how it impacts congregations is the same in all faith traditions. Using a family systems approach, John Lepper provides us with a much-needed, well-annotated, step-by-step guide for congregational leaders leading through times of ministerial transition."

J. Gregory Alexander
General Minister
Christian Church (Disciples of Christ) In Kentucky

"Rooted in solid research and the rich soil of his own experience, with this guidebook John Lepper provides able and wise guidance for congregations of a wide variety of denominations and traditions as they build bridges into the future and move forward in mission and ministry between pastors. Practical exercises and probing questions draw individuals and groups deep into exploration of congregational dynamics in ways that will both equip them for active participation in God's mission as a healthy and energetic community of faith and to identify and welcome their next pastor into that moving stream."

William O. Gafkjen
Bishop
Indiana-Kentucky Synod, ELCA

"This is an important resource for church leaders who want to guide their congregation through the critical time between pastors. Dr. Lepper's experience has given him a depth of understanding of this process, and he offers clear guidance for those who want to lead their church on a healthy path. Combining his experience in consulting and counseling, Dr. Lepper brings together valuable helps for leaders. You'll be glad to have this resource at hand."

Guy Futral
Leadership Development Team Leader, Retired
Kentucky Baptist Convention

"Lepper's insightful work can guide congregational lay leaders in 'bridging the gap' between saying goodbye and saying hello to the pastor. In this concise workbook Lepper helps congregational leaders focus on the key determinative issues of the interim between pastors. He shares his many years of experience in guiding congregations during the critical interim period between pastors. He steps in as 'virtual interim guide' to help congregational leaders address effectively the pressing issues of transition, from saying goodbye, managing anxieties and uncertainties, reclaiming congregational identity, to starting right with the new pastor. Many congregations give too much influence to professional pastoral interims while abdicating the appropriate leadership of lay leaders during the critical in-between time bracketed by losing a pastor and calling the next. Lepper's book both informs and empowers lay leaders to take responsibility for the critical work that can shape a congregation's destiny."

Israel Galindo
Dean and Professor of Christian Formation and Leadership
Baptist Theological Seminary at Richmond

"John Lepper has produced a most helpful 'bridge' for your congregation. He outlines a bridge from anxiety to trust, from an abrupt shift to a stable routine, from no pastor to a new pastor, from the wilderness to a new normal. Working through the pages of this book, your transition team will bridge the gap from what has been to what will be. And this bridge will be structurally and spiritually sound for moving into the next chapter of your congregation."

"Pastoral transitions can be filled with fear, anger, ambiguity, and confusion. This workbook helps your congregation navigate the transition by being less anxious, more hopeful, more clear, and more intentional. This book is a 'bridge' that spans the ministries of your church from what has been to what will be."

"Don't read this book; DO this book. This is not a pleasure book; this is a WORK book! John Lepper has outlined the stages of interim ministry that will lead your congregation from the pain of transition into the promise of transformation. Working through the exercises on these pages, you'll be ready to embrace your next pastoral leader with a deeper faith."

"Working through the stages of an interim ministry is often filled with fear and loss. But that doesn't have to be the case. John Lepper leads you across the 'bridge' from the fears of the interim into the faith for a bright future. The many exercises and guided conversations contained here will help you and your interim team build your own bridge from the pain of transition into the promise of transformation. This workbook will help your congregation move from resistance to readiness."

Bo Prosser
Coordinator for Missional Congregations
Cooperative Baptist Fellowship

www.ingramcontent.com/pod-product-compliance
Lightning Source LLC
Chambersburg PA
CBHW080455170426

43196CB00016B/2815